# In-house SEO Success

## 2022 EDITION

Actionable insights from industry experts,
forging your path to SEO success

We stand for SEO.

Published and compiled by

# Simon Schnieders

FOUNDER OF BLUE ARRAY

In-house SEO Success - Actionable insights from industry experts, forging your path to SEO success

ISBN 978-1-9168839-3-2

© Blue Array - Blue Array Ltd, The Blade, 3rd Floor, Abbey Square, Reading, RG1 3BE

Published in November 2022

This book is dedicated to the
incredible team at Blue Array

Simon Schnieders

# Praise for In-House SEO Success

*"Your SEO journey on steroids. This book offers you so much information and action items. From taking inspiration for the day-to-day things to taking big strategic decisions, you can now have a go-to tool in you hands"*

**Dimitris Drakatos**
Head of SEO & ASO, Paired

*"The only book that really addresses the struggles in-house SEO specialists deal with. Not only is it invaluable for anyone with an in-house SEO role, but it provides those working agency-side with unique insights into the challenges in-house SEO specialists face."*

**Steven van Vessum**
Director of Organic Marketing, Conductor

*"If you want to find relatable insights into the in-house SEO world, this is the book for you - whether you're already there or not."*

**Itamar Blauer**
SEO Manager, Cure Media

*"Creating the buy-in you need to be successful as an SEO within a large organisation can be tricky at best. That's why I highly recommend this book with real tips from real in-house SEOs."*

**Mordy Oberstein**
Head of SEO Branding, Wix

# Contents

# Foreword

Blue Array is back with another book, the third in our series, but with a new title – 'In-house SEO Success'. At Blue Array – we know that words matter – and we strive to ensure that everything we do, from our brand to our company, is for everyone. So we made this change with the aim to remove oppressive or exclusionary language from our business wherever possible.

As ever, and with two editions to look back on, we open with asking, what can the in-house SEO hope to learn from this book? This year's contributions demonstrate a shift that we've been observing over the course of this series – that SEO is becoming more professional and more skilled – and remaining a job that people want to turn up for. Many of the SEO leaders that we've spoken to have spent more than a decade showing up every day to tackle the SEO challenge of the moment – and they're still hungry for more.

SEOs are now leading brave conversations at work, about what needs to be done, who needs to be involved and how expectations have to be managed. And, also, evidencing what success can look like – and then making it happen.

It's vital for SEOs to collaborate – and doing so is creating great relationships across previously separate departments. And it's this visible willingness to reach out that is giving weight to the argument about the crucial, strategic role that SEO has for most businesses today. Even prompting some to ask for seats on the board.

Further demonstrating this growing confidence in our profession, we now see accessibility, diversity and pay becoming issues that people are confident to talk about with their peers – and their managers. We were also delighted to have a contribution from someone who took the apprenticeship route into our industry – because we know a lot of people still wonder out loud how best to support more people to join us.

We know the COVID-19 pandemic is lingering on for much longer than we would have hoped, but what this has done is challenged many businesses to do digital better. Lots have come out of this shock more willing and more able to offer great experiences for their customers. And that can often mean taking SEO much more seriously.

We know algorithm changes can still take people by surprise – but there are stories in this book about how SEOs have led their businesses to avoid future issues in this area. What we also know is that, very often, these updates can ultimately change the internet for the better – and that's better for everyone.

As usual, there are real case studies and technical discussions that give practical insights, alongside some more visionary pieces. We hope all of them offer you the inspiration to start, or keep, having brave conversations in the pursuit of great experiences for more people

Simon Schnieders (Founder)

November 2022

# Tackling a trillion-dollar opportunity – and challenge – in Latin America

## PAULA ALVAREZ
### SEARCH EXPERT, NESTLÉ

---

Paula studied communication, and discovered SEO while working on communications for an insurance company and trying to work out how to get visibility on their content. She lives in Argentina and has always worked on Spanish-speaking markets. She started at Nestlé in November 2020, brought in as a search expert, and has been dealing with strategy across 20 markets, including paid campaigns and ecommerce.

---

In Latin America, we are just discovering SEO, which for me is a positive thing. We work across Latin America – hundreds of millions of potential customers – and so there's a huge opportunity for our markets to work on SEO. And it's quite different – the way we implement our websites and the needs each market has. I work alongside Canada and the US, and the resources and the teams are different. Even the knowledge is different.

One big way that Latin America is different is, because our currency is devalued, we are suffering from inflation. And because all of the tools on the website, any developments or any updates you need to do on the website, are all paid for in dollars, budget constraint is our main challenge. So we need to be more creative in the way we develop our strategy, because it changes a lot.

Maybe you start with $10,000 a year for your strategy, but you suffer a budget cut – because the economy changes – every day. So you need to figure out how to keep working, or keep developing the strategy, because you need to keep selling your products, and you need to keep increasing your visibility. For Latin America especially, budget is the main constraint, or the main issue we need to work on. It's the most difficult part of the process.

I have a lot of stakeholders, including the local teams, and they all have their own priorities, their own goals and SEO is not always number one. And I needed to start by understanding where SEO is important – and where it's not. That means I've needed to understand the bigger picture, whether that's paid search or how to run CRM campaigns. Working as an SEO here, you need to understand the whole process.

Some of the markets I'm dealing with hadn't worked on SEO before. They may have had a website, but no one was in charge of updating or working on it. Some markets didn't even have a website online. So, we had to fix the basics and start to build from there.

# Getting creative on a limited budget

Usually, when we talk about different markets, the best approach is to have a local agency to develop the local strategy. In this case it was quite the opposite and we decided to centralise our services. So we centralised, not only the SEO strategy, but also the implementation.

We found an agency that could develop the strategy and another agency that could make the changes on the website for the same budget for the whole year. But changing or balancing the implementation, depending on what each market needs. It's cheaper for us, and also better for the agency who is in charge of managing the changes on the website, if you assure them that they will work with 10 or 20 markets the whole year and we are able to say, 'okay, we can prioritise the market'. So it is not only the budget, it's also related to the time it takes to implement. To deal with these budget constraints, there has to be flexibility on the agency side to change the amount of hours we use for each market.

In some cases, we'll need to re-assign hours or resources for the biggest markets and less to the minor markets. But for the particular markets, it means they don't need to pay more or less because we're setting up the budget at the beginning of the year. And that's it, we pay for that.

The same is true with content. We found an agency that is in charge of developing the content for all the Spanish-speaking markets and we work with them, depending on the needs or opportunity for that particular month.

Now all the markets have an SEO strategy, implementation resource and content, and that has all come with savings of between 10% and 60% of their budget, which is a lot of money for them, and obviously for us. It was centralising services that allowed us to save that money and ensure all the markets are going to benefit from SEO and web content management.

## Using existing infrastructure

One of the other interesting challenges we're dealing with is that, in many of our markets, we are the intermediary between the customer and the company making the final sale. That's because – on some of our websites – we can't sell the product directly, mainly because of the maturity of the market and/or issues with logistics.

We need to have a website so that people can find out about our products, but also so that we then send customers to retailers like Amazon or Mercado Libre and all the 'last milers'. These platforms solve a lot of issues – related to the price, the payment process and logistics, which may be impossible to resolve by ourselves.

From an SEO perspective though, it's quite challenging to drive traffic to our website – when the final destination, the sale– is through another platform. So we are trying to define and have a clear value proposition for each of our websites, because, if people are going to our website just to be redirected, that's not a good experience. For us that means, in some cases, it could be we offer promotions or discount coupons, in some cases it could be about getting people to register so they can get personalised information, depending on the objective of the website.

We've also worked on content a lot in my first year – and another challenge – which was the cannibalisation between websites. Because we are in all the Spanish-speaker markets, at the beginning, the markets sometimes copied and pasted directly from other Nestlé websites. Obviously, from an SEO point of view, that brings us a lot of indexing problems, a lot of visibility problems if, for example, in Colombia, the first results are from Ecuador.

This past year has been more negotiating, and explaining the possibilities and the improvements and the benefits of SEO. My focus is SEO, but I learned this year that, when you work with different stakeholders, different agencies, different markets and different teams inside Nestlé, you need to learn how to negotiate. Now they see that they can save money, to either reinvest in SEO or in other channels or other activities, this has allowed me to ask the markets to do other things, because they're already seeing results.

In this case, it was the money that was the number-one priority for everyone, with maybe SEO in second place. The process had to start with saving money, which came from centralisation, but that has opened the door to almost anything.

# Finding quick wins with product and data-led content

## LIMOR BARENHOLTZ
### SEO DIRECTOR, SIMILARWEB

Limor started out working on IT systems more than 20 years ago, before being appointed as a 'webmaster' and discovering that this meant they really wanted a web marketer. She worked in gaming and startups before joining McCann Tel Aviv, where she was Head of SEO Strategy and Execution for some of the biggest global brands. She's now been in-house at Similarweb for almost two years, where she's leading a team in charge of the large-scale global SEO activity for their million page website.

I love SEO, because for me, it's like 'the truth' in marketing. In other areas, there are a lot of untrue things. But with SEO, you can't really play in that way. A lot of people say it's an 'art and science' these days, and I like that, but it's become just a trendy thing to say. You certainly have to be both very onpoint and accurate in what you can actually offer, but also somehow manage to play the game of making the people click and come to your website. For me, it's an experiment, both with search engines and with people. That's why I was really happy when I said, 'I'm doing SEO and not that boring IT stuff'. Everything else seems easy to me. 'You put a little more money on that. Change the creative here'. SEO doesn't work like that and I like it. I really think it's the most trustworthy field.

I was appointed to set up Similarweb's SEO capability, and today I direct the whole SEO operation for the website for our tool, which is a tool for digital marketers and investors and salespeople. Every SEO, even if you're an agency or in-house, optimises the website of the brand they're working with. And once the basics are covered, for me, what you really want is to find places where you can create content that leans on your product's strength. Because that means it's much more trustworthy, it's much easier for you to address it and it can be very scalable. It's about finding something you can identify through data and then replicate, whether that's about creating content for A, B, C, D, E types of people, or different industries.

That's what I call 'product-led SEO', it's kind of a mix between product-marketing plans and the product itself. You're looking for something that would probably give you a lot of return traffic and will rank pretty easily, and you will be able to create more content around it easier than other things. I believe this is one of the lines of attack for SEOs right now and one that's very efficient if you manage to do it correctly.

# Making the most of your product

The Israeli national airline EL AL is one of the biggest clients for McCann. They do everything for them – TV commercials, digital, everything. And for many years their website was pure ecommerce. You come, you look for a flight, there's the flight, pay. And that worked pretty well, because they were the national airline and less flights were coming in from different airlines to Israel. But in the past few years, suddenly, every airline can go everywhere. So what we had to do is we had to find them bigger real estate. They needed to spread wider, to keep up with the whole industry.

Until then, we just had a page for each flight destination, 'flights to New York', 'flights to Amsterdam'. And so we asked, 'what do people search for when they go on vacation?'. They search for 'hotels', 'attractions', 'car rentals', 'what to do with children', 'transportation'. We actually got to a list of nine other searches that are also location related. And we just took those and replicated them over 42 destinations. It sounds pretty basic, but we gave them the journey that they didn't have on that website until then.

Now you have 'hotels in Amsterdam', 'transportation in Amsterdam', 'what to do in Amsterdam with kids', and, bam, we had 500 new pages in search and they ranked so easily. And this brought them a lot of money. Suddenly you had that 'buying engine' on every page, so someone could get to the attractions page and say 'okay, I want to go there'. It might even sound too simple, but the information wasn't there and something like that can work like magic. It gave them so much traffic and millions of extra dollars in revenue from SEO alone, it was double the previous year. We did it for so many so many brands at McCann, finding the thing that they can spin out and both easily create content on and but also help your users with task accomplishment.

At Similarweb today, we are just starting to leverage the data that we have to use. At its most basic, you can just go to our website, type in any website or app and it gives you analytics about them, for free. We have a product of data, and you can see their ranking and traffic and how much social and what audience and who are the competitors.

So we thought, 'wait, for every one of these page sections, there might be a search'. And so we did some research about it and found out that the most profitable traffic-wise, search-wise place for us to start was the world of 'alternatives to' or 'competitors of'. Because many of our users work in digital marketing or investments or sales and they look for competitors of things, often because they want to learn more about the market. Some people also look for alternatives, which might be people from the same market, but they also might be just you know normal users looking for 'alternatives to Netflix'. So we took our whole database, which has millions of websites in it, and created standalone competitor pages for each of them.

For each website today, you can go to 'xx website competitors' and you will see a list of the top 10 competitors, with similarity scores and their traffic data. It took about a year and we started to get traffic last June, slowly but surely. I played with the meta tags a little bit around January and right now these pages are getting over 500,000 visits a month. So you can search for most websites in Google, plus their competitors or alternatives, and we'll be there. Because that's what these pages do.

And moreover, these pages probably fit, in terms of search intent, to what people are looking for these days. In the past year, we've started to get traffic not only from 'website name, plus competitors', but also from 'website name' alone. Which means there are websites that Google recognises people usually search for with competitors, when they search for the name of the website. So Google doesn't even offer them our main analysis page, it sends them directly to the competitor page. That's super interesting, in terms of the 'human experiment'. It's something I'm still checking and analysing.

## Looking ahead

Already, these analysis pages are one of our most converting assets. For us, it's a lead, and it can convert people to the platform, but users can also just come and download a PDF with their website analytics. As an organisation, we have a bit of a way to go on our own measurement and conversion, but these new pages are already bringing what they need to bring, in terms of ROI. That's done, but there are at least 10 sections to the Similarweb website – we can call them 'SEO sections' or 'topic sections'. And we are now at seven or eight languages and growing. As a team leader, I get all the data, and I'm supposed to have both the granular and the holistic view. So it's my job to work out how to see all that information, for the whole website, then for each country, then each section, then each section and country. It's like a matrix.

That's where being a technical specialist, and particularly using Python, come in – because it's fast, it's very efficient and it works on Google servers. It's the best way to get everything together so you can play with it. And so now I'm off finding where our next venue can be. I have a product with a vast number of users and I've only used a small amount of data so far. What if I took one of my features and put it outside for freemium? Do people test it for a little bit and then pay? Perhaps looking at Google updates, when you have the weather and other things, what if I take something from my data and just put it outside, to get seasonal searches? So, again, it's drilling down to the value proposition of the product and seeing how many ways you can dismantle it and rebuild it. For new points of view. That's the way I see product-led SEO.

The biggest challenges, I think, these days are AI and expertise, authoritativeness and trustworthiness (EAT) type of things. EAT is not hard. It's a good concept. But the insertion of all the AI algorithms means that Google doesn't even know what's going to happen. And so as an SEO, we know less and less about how to look at our data. Because we used to understand how it behaved, and right now, no one understands how it behaves. It's a sort of a pending experiment, because this is an algorithm that learns. Right now, you have to speculate about what will happen next – and try to to be the one that's right about it.

That probably makes it even harder to get the trust that you need in the organisation. And that's something I'm trying to work on really very hard. The essence of search marketing is the fit between what we have to offer and what the user searches for, so every organisation of every size needs to understand that's where you start from – you check that any changes you make to infrastructure are going to be okay for SEO, you check your marketing plans and that there are searches behind what you're planning, before saying 'I want my product to be like that. I'll call it this and market it like this and everyone will know that's the name'. Because, as SEOs, we can easily check, 'actually, no, people don't know that's the name for this'.

I think that's our challenge – organisations need to understand that SEO is part of the infrastructure of things – that it's sophisticated and it's vital, but it's often uncertain.

# Future-proof your content with semantic SEO

## TOM BECK
### SENIOR SEO EXECUTIVE, JOHN LEWIS

Tom studied languages at university and, although this may appear a million miles from SEO, he says both require a commitment to the long term – you can't learn either overnight. After half a year at Panasonic, Tom headed to London to join an agency, where he got his first taste of SEO. Tom's first in-house role was at Photobox, where he looked after German-speaking markets, now he's at one of the UK's national institutions – 150-year-old department store John Lewis.

I really enjoyed my time at Photobox, and it was my first experience of in-house SEO, but an opportunity to join a huge brand, like John Lewis was difficult to refuse. The size of the company, and the size of the opportunities are massive, and it's certainly not what I'm used to. It's all new for me, but I'm really enjoying it. My four years in the SEO industry has flown by.

One thing that's really kept me in the industry is – there's now more of a necessity, even a requirement – to get SEO right for businesses, particularly since the pandemic. Before, it was obviously important, but the fact that people were not able to go into actual stores and had to search online, it was so important that you got those high rankings and gained as much organic visibility as possible. That was your only way of connecting with customers, really. So that's only going to continue now, that change from bricks and mortar to online shopping.

Many people will know John Lewis as one of the UK's biggest, historical institutions, and of course there was a big reliance on people visiting their stores before the pandemic. But the last couple of years have accelerated the need for SEO, and they've definitely had to increase their focus on digital marketing, and particularly search. It's one of our biggest sources of traffic and revenue now, which is brilliant. And that means there is more of an awareness across the business of the benefits of SEO.

Of all aspects of SEO, I think one that some people aren't aware of is link building – and we've actually just hired a link-building manager – who'll be working off-site and building links to our website. This role should help with building the trustworthiness and authoritativeness of our website. Of course, we have a PR team, and they're producing a lot of content on external websites. So we're really keen to make sure they know how important those follow links from high-domain authority websites are – not just for SEO, or PR – but the whole business.

One aspect of the Google algorithm that we've noticed for some of our key categories is – the bigger the assortment of products, the higher you're seeming to rank for that product – because you're more likely to be able to serve your customers' needs. So introducing new products, and also increasing our current assortment, is something that I'm working on with the buying teams, and they find that really useful. One trend we spotted during the pandemic was people looking for mini-fridges, something we'd seen an increase in search demand for over the past year or so. That's something we don't yet offer at John Lewis, but given the fact that there was this increase in search demand, it's something the SEO team put forward to the buying team. There are definitely opportunities to increase our range of current products to make sure we're meeting that customer need.

Yet, because John Lewis is a department store, it offers anything and everything – electricals, homeware and gardenware. And so, in search terms, we're having to be a source of trust on so many different fronts. That can mean producing content to go around those topics and keywords is difficult – and often brands and businesses want results straight away, but building authority, building that trustworthiness, which is vital, takes time.

I've got a good team working with me – and we're working on so many different, well-known brands – something different every hour, basically. In the past week, I've worked on sofas, menswear and electricals. It's so many different fronts that you're kind of working on, which is really exciting.

## Understanding semantic SEO

Semantic search is playing a bigger part now within SEO and it's definitely important for us at John Lewis. This is essentially how Google, Bing and other search engines are doing their best to reduce spam, and to provide the most relevant answers and a personalised user experience. It's the process that search engines use to try to understand the user intent –

the contextual meaning of your search query – in order to give you the best results, to match what you had in mind. Semantic search aims to know why you're searching for these particular keywords, and what you intend to do with the information you're receiving.

We can see it developing over the years within the Google algorithm updates – starting with Google's Knowledge Graph, where they said they wanted to create a massive online compendium, a database, to help users quickly resolve queries in the public domain. Then, in Google's Hummingbird update in 2013 – they said the biggest goal was to match users to more relevant search results by considering the user intent of the queries on a deeper level. Next was Google's RankBrain, which was all about improving how Google understands the meaning of and significance behind search queries and phrases. And then in 2019, in the BERT algorithm update, which had more to do with having the best language-processing capabilities. So it analyses the queries, words and search terms in relation to the other words present, instead of analysing each keyword.

For users, this feature is especially beneficial for getting results from longer-tail phrases, more complex grammatical search terms and voice search too, so, for example, people asking 'what are the best ways to create an SEO strategy?'. It seeks to answer users' questions, which can be quite complex, especially if they're a complete sentence, from the huge volume of voice searches made each day. So if you're writing a post about 'what is SEO?', it can be better to write sentences that contain the complete meaning, in order to increase relevancy and therefore, conversions and visits to your website. At John Lewis, a question we might look at would be 'what are the best headphones for running?', and so we're trying to produce more detailed, editorial content, to respond to it. Hence, again, the need for this larger assortment of products, which you're giving details of within that content. That could be talking about marathon running, or short-distance running – offering different headphones for different needs.

SEO TEAM

BUYING TEAM

With the development of semantic search, it's also become important to target content clusters, and not just keywords. So the keyword might be headphones, but then you want to have content surrounding the keyword – like, 'what are the best headphones running?', 'what are the best headphones for travelling?', 'what are the best headphones to get for Christmas this year?'. You want content surrounding that core keyword, because then you're showing that you're a source of trust and an authority on this topic.

Then, we'll be linking internally from that editorial content to our product pages, and that will hopefully bring conversions and increase revenue. A quick win, from a John Lewis perspective, is, we have a vast amount of product pages, so we're not necessarily able to optimise and produce the fresh content that Google prefers, as much as we want to. So, when we do see a bit of a fall in ranking for a particular product, we'll go 'okay, the content on this page hasn't been updated in a while. Maybe we could do with refreshing that', and we then see that refreshing that kind of content can play a huge part in seeing short-term gains, which is really vital for an SEO.

# How to make the most of a small in-house marketing team

## ITAMAR BLAUER

### SEO MANAGER, CURE MEDIA

Itamar is the author of Keywords for SEO and the host of the SEO Unplugged podcast. As well as being an SEO consultant and trainer, he is the SEO manager at influencer marketing agency Cure Media. As the first and only SEO at Cure, he works to ensure every marketing project combines the whole team's skills to create the best campaign for SEO, the company and its potential clients.

My first indirect SEO experience came from creating YouTube videos back in 2008, as I tried to figure out how to get people to reach my videos, organically. And then over the years, I began figuring out the same thing, but for getting websites found on Google. And I've been doing this ever since.

I've worked at an agency. I've also worked as a freelancer. And now I'm in-house. Cure Media is an influencer marketing agency, so we provide influencer marketing services to clients, specifically targeting fashion, beauty and home interior brands.

I am the SEO manager, so I'm helping them expand into the new markets and optimise the website, so that the site can perform better in these target markets for the keywords we're targeting. I didn't expect to be in the influencer marketing industry, but it's an industry that does have a lot of influence, in terms of how people shop today.

# Getting into influencing

At Cure Media – the company is only around 35 people and there's only five of us in marketing – which is quite a small marketing team. And, as the first and only SEO hire at this company – I am the SEO function. I know a lot of brands and companies will have in-house teams of 20 or 30 SEO people. So there is a big difference in that.

There are three co-founders of the company – and they all understand the work that I do – and they see the value there. Joining a company that understands the value of something like SEO, even before you've got someone on board, can be really important. They understand it's a channel that can take time, it's a channel where there's a lot that goes into it. It's not like something so quick and easy as running a paid campaign with a set budget.

Every month or so, we do a 'lunch and learn', and a couple of months after I joined, I did one on SEO, just so everyone in the company knows what SEO is, and the kind of stuff that I'm doing. People seemed to really value that. And I think everyone's pretty on board with everything that we're doing. We all understand what our strengths are. The whole company, I think, is on board.

## Playing to your strengths

Because we're a small team, it means that there's more creative freedom, we have the ability to do experiments. At Cure, they say 'if you have an idea, and you think it can work, do it'. If I was at another company, where ideas would have to go through multiple people, it might take a lot longer. So we are really efficient, even though we've got a smaller team. We also really make the most out of what we can bring to the table, individually.

Of course, on the SEO side of things, the same things still apply. You've still got to understand what people are looking for, you've still got to understand what sort of content resonates with that, and be able to satisfy what a user might be searching for.

But I'm able to go and speak to the head of sales and say, 'okay, what are their pain points? What are they struggling with?'. I'm using the sales team because they get loads of questions from brands that contact them about all of these things. Or, if we need help in terms of 'well, how do we address this issue?', we can talk to operations, because they do everything day to day, they have an enormous amount of knowledge.

We've got our own tech team, dedicated campaign managers, people who have created great processes and tech, and the ability to analyse influencer campaigns. And we've got all this historical data that not many people will have. So that all helps feed into the content that we're writing – we're utilising all of these different areas in the company to be able to create extremely comprehensive and useful content for our target audience.

Once I get this kind of information, it becomes a lot easier for us as a marketing team to come up with content that helps match that. The content we create is basically education – it's useful for brands who want to do influencer marketing, just so they're educated about the strategies you could go for, and they get a good understanding of what they should do.

We've got people who are excellent at writing content, excellent at creating graphics, excellent at producing videos. And that's why the content that we produce is extremely comprehensive. If we've covered a topic, we might have a blog post, we might have a webinar, we might have a podcast episode on it, we might have a couple of YouTube videos. And of course, we make sure we've optimised the content and done outreach.

All of that, in the SEO sense, is showcasing that we've got the authority within these topics, and again, it's stuff that's very relevant for our ideal target audience. That means we're also able to build some incredible links, essentially, by unifying our individual expertise into content that is industry-leading and engaging.

Some of the links we get for each campaign come proactively from outreach, but we're also able to get great links that come through how well the content is performing in search. Because it's ranking well, these websites want to use this as a reference.

And this just shows the results that you can get when you unify your teams, and have a marketing team where people bring different people skills and combine them into one piece of great content.

# Keyword pioneering

The content we're building is all around showing our expertise and hitting the sort of things that people would want to be looking for now or even in the future. That's something I call 'keyword pioneering' – essentially looking at terms that maybe aren't mainstream now, but being thought leaders, we know they are going to become a lot more popular in the next few years.

So for example, at Cure Media, we talk about influencer marketing being 'data-driven' and going for 'always-on' influencer campaigns. And that's something we've seen more and more people talking about. When I went to the Influencer Marketing Show in London last year, there were people speaking about that. And there were loads of brands there and that means more people are going to be looking for that sort of thing.

From our side of things, that's great, because we've been actually doing this and we've got content that supports that. For a while now, we've been able to really push our thought leadership and expertise around this topic. Spending this time, being useful, helping the industry progress and helping brands achieve great results, that's what our goal is.

# Making the most of it

The biggest challenge is expanding our capabilities when it comes to the scale. SEO is a marketing function that works best when you have a team of dedicated technical developers, content writers, digital PR outreach, link builders, and overall SEO strategists.

But we're not an SEO team at Cure. So it can be difficult to scale up a strategy, or you could use up too much of your marketing team's time when they've got lots of other projects going on that don't revolve around SEO. That's why it's important to prioritise the most critical SEO projects and activities that will benefit SEO without bombarding your colleagues' calendars too much with things that are purely seen as an SEO.

And of course, I try to bring as much SEO benefit as I can to our other marketing activities. You have to work with what you have, and prioritise, to be able to get the results by doing the most important things. There is, of course, a lot to do, and there's only so much of our time that we can use up.

My biggest advice – if you want to become an in-house SEO – is to get a solid understanding of the current marketing team and what their strengths are. If you're being interviewed for an SEO role in-house, then you should be asking what the current marketing team looks like. Just so you know what each person's role is and what they're good at. So that you can say, 'okay, this person is great at creating video content, so could be utilising that in every single blog post to make it more engaging, or we could put up some schema for videos'.

You can find ways to unify a marketing team and use other people's expertise to help you execute a successful SEO strategy. After all, teamwork makes the (SEO) dream work.

# Here's the empathy in SEO

## JAMES-CHARLES CONNINGTON
### UK AND EU SEARCH AND ORGANIC GROWTH LEAD, PHILIP MORRIS INTERNATIONAL

---

JC has worked for some of the most recognisable in-house brands, spanning from Casio to Cancer Research UK. He recently moved to head up UK SEO for Philip Morris International, and is now committed to helping the near-200-year-old cigarette company and its customers finally go smoke free. He's also worked agency-side, loves open-sea swimming and surfing, and had a previous career in a rock band, which achieved a number-two single in the UK.

---

There's a book called Emotional Intelligence by Daniel Goleman, which came out in the 90s, and it is all about the different ways that people think, react, and let's say – search. In my role today, I'm thinking about alternatives to smoking, and if someone's searching for that, it suggests that they are interested in changing their behaviour.

But there's something around that search that says they're looking for something else, that they don't have enough information to make a decision right now. Google calls this the 'messy middle' of the funnel and it's an area that I've become increasingly interested in. The 'messy middle' is made up of people who are past making that initial investigation or search, where they might not really know what they're looking for.

They might have seen an advert, a campaign on TV or radio. And they're starting to search for something to help them perhaps take that next step. That means SEOs like me need to provide content and information to meet that need, and to allow them to make a better and more informed choice. That may be a piece of content to shape opinion which can help them on the consideration journey.

But, for me, it's the principle of empathy in SEO that is vital to bringing about that behavioural change. This isn't about trying to lead a horse to water and get it to drink – it's more about examining the context of the search – where in that journey are they? Have they had touch points with us on other channels? If they have, what kind of content do we need to provide that will resonate with them now?

And for me, we're being empathic in doing that. We're not just using words and content design to do that, but we're also using data to give us an idea of what problem that user is trying to solve now. How can we help them clear a hurdle in their life or make a change in their behaviour that might hopefully be a positive change? And whether it's Cancer Research or Phillip Morris, there are similarities in this approach.

It's quite interesting, because it's actually hard to create loads of content for the messy middle, and there's not much advice about it, like 'how do you bring people in straight to the middle of the funnel? Or take them from the top to the middle?'. Because often you can take from the top to convert. That's the shortest route for conversion. And that's essentially what we're all looking for. How can we take someone from A to B in the shortest time possible, right?. That's what our employers want us to help enable.

But actually, sometimes, it's worth being empathic and saying, 'well, actually, in this sales journey, if it's something around wills, (which is something I was involved with at Cancer Research UK), that's going to take people a bit of time'. That's a big decision, it's a big investment. It's about their life. So we shouldn't just have that 'growth hat' on, and think, 'right, what's the shortest route?'. We want to empathise with them and say, 'well, we understand this is not something you're going to decide right here right now, this week, this month'. So you have to look at that lifecycle, at the journey, and try to make your content align with that, allow them that space and make your content reflect that.

## Asking the right questions

Creating change isn't easy – we may be looking at behaviour that someone's had for 20, 30, 40, 50 years – and asking people to move to a more environmentally friendly product, for example. But for a good SEO who wants to employ empathy, there are four questions you can ask to help you get started.

The first question is, 'how can we change how people feel?'. The second question is, 'how does our product or service shift the way they're feeling, so that they're ready to decide to do or buy something new?'. The third question is 'what do they believe?' Or more specifically 'what do they believe about what they're currently doing or using?'. So if they're using that plastic and metal Gillette razor, what can our content do to move them from that habit of 20 years to looking at a fully biodegradable, less harmful and more sustainable product? This is where you can use content that's more generally about sustainability and what good it does, you can preface stuff with that, rather than writing a hard sell.

There are so many people in our industry, especially in the field of UX, who moan about the long scroll. But actually, people do spend time on longer content. And this is another area of empathy. We need to allow people the space and the time to make these decisions. That means not being afraid to write relevant, useful, helpful content that guides people, that informs people to make these changes, by answering those questions.

The last question is, 'what belief do people have already about us?'. For me in my previous role at Cancer Research – we had a reputation. I'm now at PMI – and we have a reputation. So what pre-existing ideas do people have – and are there barriers there? So we've not just got to think 'I have a product page and a category page', or 'I have a service that my client or the organisation I work for wants to create a campaign for', etc. This is a multi-channel consideration, where you can also be considering creatives for PPC or display, and asking whether all the output is helping to answer these questions.

A big thing right now in SEO, that doesn't get termed as 'empathy', but I believe it is, is matching the language we use in our content to match user needs. I think we should always look to echo customer language. A lot of businesses tend to write inaccessible, jargonistic, business-led copy, and it's about working with your content team to try to find the empathic way to talk about these things. Something that's really related, and also key for the industry right now, is accessibility. This is also about caring about people and their experience.

One thing that might help here is taking a look at how customers are already talking about your products or your business. Look at the reviews, look at this stuff on social media, your Facebook page. What are people saying about you? And think about using the positive language they use in your copy, on the blog, on the category page or on the product page. Often what people are saying is a goldmine of information.

# Spreading empathy in-house

This idea of empathy doesn't just stop at what we can do as SEOs. A large part of it is realising that the SEOs, the UX team, the content strategists, the web devs, the engineers – the people we work alongside and place demands upon – are all essentially after one thing, which is giving users and customers a good digital experience.

And when you realise that, that's when you realise actually, there are so many insights that the devs are going to have about functionality and barriers to transact. The UX team, from looking at tools like Hotjar, knows how people are moving around on our pages. So make sure you allow yourself time to sit down, for a day, an afternoon, or an hour with them. What were their pain points last quarter, last month? Is there anything you can do?

You'll soon realise that being empathic and listening to other teams' pain points, rather than just having your 'SEO hat' on, really helps with what we're all trying to do. Of course, we're all after the same thing, which is growth, conversions, good reviews, retention, happy customers.

# A buyer's guide for the 'messy middle'

A really good example of content that hits that messy-middle sweet spot is a 'buyer's guide' for a product. Dan Shure is someone who advocates creating them, and the fact that a lot of SEOs don't create them means it's one of those untapped things, which I would definitely recommend, for a few reasons.

Firstly, if you're looking to bring people in and not cannibalise from your other pages, there's evidence Google can actually disambiguate between a buyer's guide and a product page. It recognises them as a legitimate way to bring people into the middle of the funnel.

Secondly, then, you've got loads of space to share the USPs of the product, the information that the business wants you to put in, sustainability stuff – which is important because a lot of people care about that these days. Thirdly, you're giving people a longform piece of content, one page, maybe an accompanying PDF, because Google can rank those too.

And finally you're saying this is 'one-stop shop, exhaustive content', and Matt Cutts, the former Google software engineer, likes that. He's said he likes content to be guided and exhaustive and helpful. That's what a buyer's guide is.

Obviously, you want to use relevant links from the guide to take people to the product or category pages. But buyer's guides are a really effective way of creating great content to match that messy-middle demand.

# How to go from zero to millions in traffic – and what you might do next

## DIMITRIS DRAKATOS

### HEAD OF SEO AND ASO, PAIRED

From UK fintech unicorn Revolut to Peanut app, which was one of the 'Apple Best' of 2021, Dimitris has worked at some of the most interesting digital-first brands. A passionate digital marketer and organic growth lead, he is a Reforge alumnus, has spoken at industry conferences such as BrightonSEO and Measurefest, is a mentor at GrowthMentor and FemTech Lab, and is a judge at the Drum Awards for Search. Dimitris has recently joined couples app Paired to lead on search and app-store optimisation.

I joined Peanut in October 2020 and had to build everything from scratch. It is a great business, however, SEO wise, there was nothing being done prior to my arrival. The good thing is, the C-suite has a strong belief in SEO, which is always a big deal for us. At the same time, working at a Series A company, with around 15 people at the time, can be pretty chaotic.

When I arrived, we had to outsource everything, and at the same time, make sure that we weren't overspending. But one of the big pain points was that the competitors we have in search had been investing in SEO for several years, so they had huge domain authority. So the big challenge for us was, how can we be among them, to take some piece of that pie, sooner, if we haven't been around for the long term?

I'm delighted to say that we've gone from zero to 2.3 million organic monthly visits in just 12 months – which was a huge milestone – initially using a strategy called 'publishing velocity' SEO, where we decided to publish a lot of articles and try to close that big gap as quickly as possible.

## Publishing velocity

To get started I took the main keyword we were targeting – and you can add this to a tool like Semrush or Ahrefs – and looked at the top-ranking page for this keyword. And, while the top result is not ranking just for this keyword, but also a lot of very close variations, this gives you the traffic potential, or the total organic traffic for this page on a monthly basis. If you want to cover five keywords, you have 'X' number of traffic potential. If you want to cover 100 keywords, the traffic potential increases a lot. So my approach, since we wanted to close this big gap between our search competitors quickly, was to increase this traffic potential.

Now say you're writing five articles and you have a success rate – where success means, let's say, being in the top five results – that may be 20%. (So one out of five articles would feature in the top five SERPS results).

If you do 100 articles, and assuming that we don't have the 20% success rate, you might have like a 15% or even a 10% rate, it's still much higher traffic compared to a 20% success rate on five articles.

So instead of just writing five or 10 articles on a monthly basis, we started with 40, went to 50, and for some months, we were delivering around 100 articles. So our traffic potential was huge. The more keywords we were covering, the more we were increasing our chances of getting higher numbers and more traffic.

That's why I'm also a big fan of topic clusters. Instead of just trying to rank for random keywords, you're clustering the keywords and the content you produce, so that you can create topical authority. This is also important, because the more keywords you cover, the faster you cover the topic. Instead of just having 10 keywords in one cluster and trying to cover them in a three-month period, you're covering one in the first month, so you have more topic clusters to cover in the next. That means, instead of aiming to have one topic cluster completed in one quarter, we could have three or four.

This strategy creates a domino effect, and, in this case, we were increasing our topic authority a lot, but also our internal linking, because we were linking between very relevant articles. That means we're also improving our indexability and credibility. Of course, domain authority plays a big role. However, the most important thing is to provide great content, with great content comes authority. What we've seen with Peanut is – without doing any off-page SEO, at least in the first year – because we have delivered great content and a great amount of content, we've seen a spike in backlinks. Other websites are finding our articles on the first page, and are then just grabbing information and mentioning us. The greatest strategy of all for me is delivering unique, informative content that really answers the searcher's intent.

# Driving product development

To deliver this strategy, we had to grow our team. That included outsourcing, and the agency we were working with grew as our business grew, so they hired more writers to handle the demand. And we also hired another great SEO content writer in-house. But interestingly, and very importantly, getting this huge amount of organic traffic, this demand, has created an appetite for the business to go from being an app-only business to having a new, lighter web-version.

At the beginning, the idea of creating a web version of Peanut was a very controversial topic. Some people thought that, considering the amount of resources that would need to be used to deliver this, the return on investment, financial investment or time spent, wouldn't be that good. But I was a big believer in the web version.

Sometimes brands just don't think about alternatives and it was the same when I was at Revolut, where I was selling the same thoughts some years ago. And the thing is, it's not just about improving the conversion rate from an organic-acquisition perspective, it's about helping people with their needs. So maybe a person wants to join Peanut, for example, but she doesn't want to download the app, do the selfie verification, or she doesn't want to do it now. She just wants an answer, so downloading the app, or doing the verification, can add more friction.

It's about the user experience. Imagine if you're stuck on your laptop, and you still want to use a great product, having this option, even if it's not the best experience, even if it's not this portable experience you have on your mobile, it can still be a good user experience. The more digital products are evolving, and the more competition is exploding, the more likely you have to play this card as well. We already have two engineers dedicated to the web, along with a product owner, a web-marketing person and a web designer. So instead of splitting our resources, we've got a fully weaponised web team to support the growth.

# Driving business growth

When you start out, and the business is pretty immature in terms of SEO and organic traffic, you have to sit down and completely understand the product, the pain points, the USPs, everything. However, the more established you become in terms of traffic – and the more traffic you bring – the more data you have.

The next stage of your approach is to make sure you're not just bringing a huge amount of traffic, but also trying to convert this traffic. At the end of the day, companies don't care about the number of keywords you're targeting or total organic traffic – they care about instals, leads, sales and revenue. These are the numbers the C-level speaks about.

So, after one year, apart from continuing to increase our traffic, we're also performing conversion-rate optimisation. And it's about analysing the data, and performing A/B tests to see how we could differentiate the call-to-action, the placements, everything that could impact the conversions. We started with a pretty low conversion rate, which makes sense, because the website wasn't built for acquisition purposes, it was just mentioning, 'we are Peanut, we do this, here's the story and if you want to, download the app from the App Store or Play Store'. And then we'd created an organic-acquisition machine, so we had to make sure that we revisited the UX.

Also, with the Core Web Vitals going live, with the new official ranking factors for Google, page experience is crucial. So we needed to make sure that we had a great score there, that we're not just writing articles, but providing the best user experience. After several tests, we tripled the conversion rate, which, if you check in plain numbers, it's still kind of small. However, it's a small percentage of a huge amount of traffic. So it still makes a great difference.

We have two factors that make us really optimistic. One is, we keep growing our traffic. Secondly, we keep doing A/B tests and conversion-rate optimisation. We're aiming to keep increasing these two variables

simultaneously. So at the end, we will have more and more conversions. And this is how everything ties together. Adding the lighter-weight version of the app will definitely create more conversions, because, again, even if you're a mobile or desktop, you visit an article, you learn about Peanut, you say, 'oh, it's a great product, let's try it'. But you don't just have to download the app on the App Store, maybe some people are not on the wifi, or they don't have enough phone memory.

What I've realised, and probably like a lot of SEOs, is the more good results you bring, the more you increase the appetite from everyone inside the company. So when I started we'd say, 'we're gonna deliver 90,000 monthly organic visits', and everyone would be happy. Now that we have around 2.5 million, some people say, 'oh, maybe we could push more and more and more'. It makes sense, you know, the more food you're bringing, the more appetite you create.

And so the big bet for us is how we can maintain and grow this channel. And how we can also make sure that, while we're growing, we're also not losing conversions. We're bringing relevant traffic and translating this traffic into users. So this is the big bet for us this year, how we can maintain this really big channel that we have created in a short period, and make sure we're getting the most of it.

It's challenging, you know, because we're a young team, we're a Series A company. But we have a very noble mission ultimately – which is helping women across all their life stages.

# Stop wasting Google's time by streamlining your crawl budget

## ALINA GHOST

SEO MANAGER, DEBENHAMS AT BOOHOO GROUP

---

Alina started out working for someone who said she was doing
SEO – but she probably wasn't. She was eventually picked up by
Carpetright in 2012, where she learned the real SEO basics alongside
the company's external agency. Then in 2014, Alina went to work
at Debenhams for the first time, doing link building and technical
content work as an SEO assistant. After consultancy roles at Tesco
and the BBC, then working in-house at a luxury interiors brand
AMARA, and having a baby, she's back at Debenhams, now owned
by Boohoo, where she's really embraced the technical aspects.

---

Imagine a startup. I know it's a weird thing to say – that Debenhams is a startup. But after Boohoo bought Debenhams in 2021, they only had a few weeks to redesign the website. Imagine trying to get a website, for this mammoth brand, and basically migrate it during that time. That was a challenge in itself – and I came on about a week before we actually migrated.

There was this completely new website – and at one point, we didn't even have metadata – so for us, it was about getting the basics sorted and working on the smart stuff at the same time. But because we're such a good brand, historic, quite old, everybody knows about us, a lot of these things were accelerated.

I love that I was able to come back to Debenhams, as SEO manager, because I started there as an SEO assistant so many years ago. And we are very lucky now to be a part of the Boohoo group, who have SEOs for other brands, so we do work a little bit like an agency sometimes, where we come together and share knowledge.

The fact that I was able to put that strategy together really excited me. The fact that I was able to come back to this brand that I know so well and know the product, know the audience, and basically put my own spin on it to help this brand out. There's that personal stake in there. It's been a crazy year, but also very exciting, because we are seeing that organic growth back, slowly but surely.

# Getting technical

I actually taught myself a lot of the technical areas of SEO, while building my own blog and websites. I just played around with them, because I needed to understand how that code fits together and is implemented, in order for the search engine to understand your content better. So that's where it started off.

For me it comes down to a few key areas really – content, the technical aspects of your website and user experience. So, for example, if you're creating really good content, but the search engine can't find it, because your website isn't technically sound – you need to lead yourself into that technical area.

This leads into more complex things, like international migrations, as I did in my previous role at AMARA, and understanding the taxonomy of the website. Sitemaps are also super important. In the past year, we've been doing them manually for Debenhams, but have recently moved on to a product-automation sitemap.

Then it moves on to the whole UX thing. Because I've been working in ecommerce and in-brand this past decade, facets and filters have been a really big priority as well.

But for me, crawl budget is a really huge part of technical SEO – ultimately search engines have a finite amount of time to spend crawling your website to understand it – and you don't want to waste it. So doing work on this will help you, and the search engines, understand what pages are important.

## Understanding your crawl budget

Firstly, get as many tools as you can to crawl your website and understand what pages are being seen. You can use a tool that's quite cheap, like Screaming Frog, or something more sophisticated, like Deepcrawl or Botify. What status do the pages have? Is it a 200? Meaning the page request has been understood and accepted. Is it a redirection? Or is it a 404? So it doesn't exist.

Then you can marry that information up with log files. Log files are a really good way of understanding exactly when, and what bot, has seen what page. By doing crawls of your website, and looking at log files, you're able to understand and marry up what search engines are seeing compared to what you want them to see. And vice versa, in the sense that, you can block some areas of your site. So for example, the customer login and account areas should usually always be blocked, because you don't want them to see that customer information (it's against GDPR as well.)

However, not a lot of people have their log files, because it is very technical, and it's a lot of data in one file. My recommendation would be to go and have a look at that as quickly as possible, as soon as you can. So essentially looking at that information, you can then figure out – are these bots looking at pages that you don't want them to see?

If that's the case, you can use your robots.txt file to exclude them, so disallow a section. You can do wildcards in the query, or you can use one URL to get them removed from search engines. What we're doing here is just making sure that time, that is so valuable, is spent on the right areas. Robots.txt is probably number one, and probably the quickest thing to implement, from a technical perspective.

Then – it's also looking at your sitemaps. These are like the fundamentals of having a website. You're giving a list to a search engine and say, 'have a look at all of these pages because they're really important'. You can give them priorities, although it's questionable whether they actually are used. Nonetheless, you can tell a search engine, 'look, you can have a look at this whole list because these pages are very important to us'. You can break sitemaps down to images, categories and products as well.

The reason that's really good is because you can also feed that sitemap into Google Search Console directly, so that they don't get missed. That's a really quick win – a quick way of getting that time focused on the pages that are important to you.

How do you find those URLs and that information? Well, you use Screaming Frog, or anything more sophisticated, just to understand what pages you actually have on your website. Is there anything that is missing off the sitemap? That doesn't mean that Google will not go and have a look at it. If a search engine finds it another way, they can still find it and they can still index it.

Another quick way to focus on your crawl budget is by adding parameters to Google Search Console to exclude them from the index. This is mostly related to tracked links or affiliate ones, where you know these shouldn't be indexed and rather must be canonicalised to the main page. Essentially, parameters are usually anything after a question mark in your URL, and they usually suggest tracking – whether it's affiliate tracking, whether it's an Urchin Tracking Module (UTM), like a Google track link, or similar. There are plenty of areas where we might want to use a tracked link or a parameter.

You can actually remove those from your Google crawl budget by adding them into Google Search Console this way – if the canonicalisation is correct – to indicate which is your main page, for example. Anything with an additional parameter, we don't actually need to have crawled, because the pages are exactly identical. In effect, we are removing these parameters from Google's search list and saying, 'don't look at this, don't look at affiliate track links, don't look at UTM use'. This means we are consolidating all of that authority into your main page.

Another one on the list will be around crawl rates and the percentage of your pages that are 200s – those that are working correctly – versus having a lot of 404s, 301s and redirections and stuff. Within the settings area of Google Search Console, you can also see how many times Google sees all these pages and when there are too many that aren't working. Essentially, this is telling you 'look at how many pages we've had to look at in the past 30 days – this is the percentage of them that are 200s'. If you have a lot of any one particular one that is not a 200 – go investigate.

So when you do a crawl, if you've got a lot of pages with a 404, have a think about why they are 404 in the first place. Do you expect them not to be there? Why do the pages not exist? Secondly, why is there no redirect to a relevant page? Have a look at what you can do there because that is affecting your crawl budget – essentially – if they are seeing a lot of 404s, you're telling them that your website is not maintained, not looked after, you don't have relevant content and you're wasting their time.

And what happens over time is that search engines get tired of your website, so much so that they stop coming to you as much. Have a think about adding 301 redirects to useful pages rather than serving 404s.

The next step to consider, and something that the Debenhams new website has, is a lot of JavaScript. We know that's like the 'new thing to use' – the React JavaScript library is good because you can plug APIs into it and you can use JavaScript coding to showcase information that you want to highlight. That brings issues, however, from an SEO point of view, in relation to your crawl budget.

One aspect is that, when there is JavaScript, something that needs to be done for it to be processed and understood ready for the user, is rendering. If that's done via search engine, they waste a lot of time doing that. This can mean, potentially, those pages even go into a queue of up to five days, I've heard. So your content might not be seen for a long time – and it can't be indexed if they can't see that information. So what you need to do is improve your rendering, by making sure that it's done server side – before it gets to the search engines, before it gets to the user.

JavaScript is notorious for taking a long time to process – which, if not addressed, eats into your crawl budget and performance. By consolidating some things and improving the JavaScript code, to make it work a little bit smarter, you can improve your page load times. This means, if it's only a quick time for a search engine to have a look at your pages, it then can go on to a different page. So essentially, you're improving your crawl budget that way so that they can spend more time on more pages. Don't get me started on how the slowness of your site affects user experience!

Last but not least are your taxonomy and internal linking. This is about telling a search engine the importance of a page – which is also great for users. That's usually focussed on your top menu and is about understanding the main pages you have, what kind of categories of products you're selling, what categories you're going to showcase and the subcategories underneath.

By ensuring that you have a hierarchy of pages, and internal linking to these pages, you're giving that popularity information to the search engines. So, like an upside-down tree, the homepage gets 100% of the authority, any categories underneath then get a distribution of that, let's say five categories, which means they get 20% of that authority each, the subcategories underneath those then distribute the 20%. Because of the clicks each page is away from the homepage – this helps search engines and users – find your pages, as well as understanding how important they are.

Ultimately, at Debenhams today, we want it to be a one-stop shop for people – and the real challenge for us is understanding how we please everybody, especially when there are such high expectations around this historic brand. We're now working more on the UX side of things – filtering optimisation, which isn't directly SEO, but does have a huge impact on our work.

# A future-proof SEO strategy at Future

## SIMON GLANVILLE
### HEAD OF SEO, FUTURE

---

Simon studied journalism at university and got his break through a government-backed internship when he graduated, which was extended from 10 weeks to 18 months after he successfully went to 'get some traffic'. He says his first 'proper job' in SEO came when he joined Vouchercloud. After three years of great SEO success – the company was hit by a Google algorithm update that cost traffic and revenue. But, after 12 months clawing things back, they eventually sold to Groupon. He's been at Future for four years.

---

At Future, our technical SEO team works across three areas, one is growing traffic from our existing sites, the second is migrating sites over to our core platform and the third is iterating on that platform. The team is split into two, so operations is more the technical side, and then we've got audience development.

In terms of audience development, new content is huge for us. This team is doing 'gap analysis', looking at what we should be writing about next, what our competitors are doing, what's spiking, what people are looking for. Some of our sites are publishing hundreds of posts a day. It's a balancing act, because we also have a lot of evergreen content that has been around for a while, most of which needs to be regularly updated to prevent it becoming out of date. That could be a buying guide, a review, not necessarily a news story. Someone used the analogy the other day, 'if you go to a supermarket, you want your freshest stuff at the front'. Then it's the stuff in the backlog that you've got to worry about, whether that's 'gone off', or causing a problem.

From a technical point of view, we don't just focus on the new content but also the older content that could be playing a part in our rankings. Do we clean it up, or do we leave it? Some of our sites have been around for 10, 15, even 20 years, and have a lot of content, but some of it might be thin, or not even relevant to the site anymore. A lot of these sites have been around for so long, they haven't necessarily been audited or tidied up. I'm a big believer that everything that is in the index counts towards site quality, so we review all of our content with that in mind.

There have historically been sites that always had a problem from Google core algorithm updates, which can be done two to four times a year, but we've turned them around. It does take a lot of work to rectify, especially on big sites, where there's a huge amount to do. We had sites that had been really struggling for over a year and we did a lot of work to get them going in the right direction.

Typically, you would see some sites that have big jumps and big drops in traffic. From my experience, that's because they're sites that have everything indexed, without really being careful with it. We used to be quite reactive when this happened, perhaps going in and taking lots of content out of the index. We are now a lot more proactive. That might be no-indexing certain things, removing and redirecting others, or suggesting updates to editorial teams.

We've got some really big sites and now we are quite careful about what we let Google index. Everything that Google indexes counts towards site quality. I've worked on sites in the past where we've kind of let everything be indexed and that's bitten us, but we quite regularly review our bigger sites to find out if there is content that we could remove. We'll consider different metrics, things like 'does that URL get any traffic? Does it get any impressions? Does it rank for any keywords at all?'. And if the answer is no to those, and it's really old, it might be irrelevant to the site, so that's the sort of thing that we might no-index.

But, it's fair to say that we're still quite cautious. We don't want to take a sledgehammer to a site, because that content could also be helping it to rank. I always give the example where we'd written about the iPhone 4 and wondered whether to just get rid of that content. I argued that, although people aren't necessarily searching for that now, that content shows a search engine, especially, that you're an expert. Old content can also have strong signals from both external and internal links, so we look at that too to help inform decisions.

We also link to all of our article content through an archive – effectively a HTML sitemap – which is mainly for the benefit of search engines, so they can easily find all of our content. A user could also go through and look at all the TechRadar posts from January 2010, for example, but not all of that would be included in Google's index.

## Getting SEO on everyone's agenda

At Vouchercloud, we were pre-warning our c-level that there were issues that we needed to fix in order to prevent us being hit by a Google update – not least because organic search was more than 50% of our revenue.

But because SEO was always doing quite well there, it perhaps seemed like everything would be fine. As soon as we did get hit, of course, the changes that we'd been asking to make for six months happened, immediately. But it was too late and it takes time for search engines to take any changes into account. That was a big moment where I realised that I needed to be more forceful. So I've taken that experience with me to Future.

Coming into a publishing house, I've never seen anything like it, where there's hundreds of websites and hundreds of writers. From an SEO perspective, I wasn't sure whether content was vetted, how you could possibly create a process for that. Future is a well-oiled machine, but when I first started, as is quite typical, you would see people make changes to things without thinking about SEO. Then they would come to you to see if you could fix it. And sometimes when that happens, it's almost too late, Google has already seen it and they might have made changes as a result.

But I've learned to be a lot more vocal if I think we need to make a change. I try to use case studies shared by other businesses to show what we need to do and what might happen if we don't. Today, we do a lot of training with editorial teams about the importance of SEO and produce playbooks for them. That means we're now getting to the point where people will come to us and say, 'we want to make this change, what's the SEO impact? Should we think about this differently?'.

They all ask the right questions – they'll get ranking reports, they're looking at keywords, but also thinking about the bigger picture in terms of topic clusters – and it works because it's not a siloed SEO team, you can't have success that way. We've set up Slack channels for SEO and we actually see editorial teams answering each other's questions. Our CEO even does a weekly email where she'll often be talking about SEO. If you've got the CEO talking about SEO, and understanding its importance, then that is a big thing. That's when you know you're getting somewhere, when the whole business is thinking about SEO.

## An SEO-driven future at Future

SEO is a massive part of our core platform – how it's set up, how it's built. And we will likely be iterating forever on the platform. We're constantly meeting with the developers, going through different things. But another big part of our plans at Future are acquisitions. This is because we're focussed on a 'one, two, three' strategy. So not just, 'can we get rank number one?', but actually, 'can we rank one, two and three?'. As an SEO, ranking one is pretty good. But we've been tasked with dominating the whole SERP. In the tech vertical now, for example, we might have five or six sites that are competing for the same keywords on page one of Google, and sometimes we'll get five or six sites on page one.

We acquired TI Media in early 2020 and Dennis Publishing towards the end of 2021 – both of which had sites that fit our strategy. So, where we might have already had a site in these verticals, now we might have three or four. When we buy these companies, the sites essentially go into a big queue to get them onto our platform. So, where we were doing about four or five migrations a year, which in itself is not small, we now need to do more than double that. It's a big ask because there are times of year – such as Black Friday or Christmas – where we don't move sites. You don't want to move a site when it's getting most of its traffic.

It's a lot of work, from my team's point of view, it takes a lot of time and a lot of our day to day. And migrations for an SEO are stressful at any time – it's a bit like moving house – something can always go wrong. Plus, some of these websites are quite large, so when moving them to different platforms, there's lots of intricacies, and things that you have to map and make sure are correct.

What we want to do eventually is get every site on our core platform. The reason for that is, firstly, we do a lot of work on that platform and from an SEO point of view, we think it's best in class. And, because SEO is always changing, you're constantly trying to make improvements to the platform to make it better. Secondly, it monetises better than a lot of other platforms. So from an advertising perspective, even from an affiliate point of view, it makes more money. We've literally moved sites over to the platform and, while traffic has stayed the same, the revenues increased straightaway.

Normally, when you migrate a site, it's a success if it doesn't drop in traffic, you're content keeping the status quo and getting it in a good place for long-term growth. But we've had sites that have moved over without any new content and have really improved in traffic almost instantly. A recent example is a site we migrated at the back-end of last year that saw an immediate improvement after the migration. The site admittedly had a lot of content that we cleared up as part of the migration, and was coming from a platform with a number of technical issues and limitations, but is now posting record traffic numbers and continues to go from strength to strength.

# Why SEOs have to commit to great storytelling

## DANIEL HARRISON
### HEAD OF ORGANIC GROWTH, HEYCAR

Daniel has been working on websites for more than two decades – and has spent all of that time in the automotive sector, starting at legacy publishing brand Parkers. Here, he worked with a team that transformed it into a digital-first title. He joined Honest John as editor in 2009, where he applied his journalism training to the task of developing its editorial proposition, with a keen eye on search. Dan became editorial director in 2015, and the company had significant success with data-driven products and reader-focussed services. It was bought by heycar in 2020, where he is now head of organic growth for the company's UK website portfolio.

I've been working on websites since before SEO was even a thing – 21 years now – at that time, people were still saying, 'how do search engines generate revenue? Aren't the internet and Google just passing fads?'. It sounds a bit ridiculous now, but when I first started at Parkers, it was just accepted that your website would be on that first page of the search results. But, over time, there was much more competition. National and local newspapers suddenly caught on, and started publishing car-related content. Then car dealers started to set up their own content operations. So after a few years, it was becoming a bit more difficult to come up at the top of that search page – suddenly everyone was a website or 'SEO expert'.

I discovered early in my career that there's crossover between the core foundations of good journalism and good SEO – the two don't need to compete – achieving one is the same as achieving the other. Good journalism is about being economical with words – choosing them very carefully – and getting your message, facts and key takeaways within the first couple of paragraphs. For SEO, that translates to getting the right keywords in and making sure the piece is easy to digest, whether that's for a search engine or a human being.

But I've always had a people-first approach to content. There is little point in writing with the aim of pleasing a search engine – having content ranking well isn't the final destination – it is not the end user, real people are. So you have to do the right thing by them by providing the very best editorial you can – ideally with a bit of insight that's unavailable elsewhere. If your site has built authority and is technically sound, you will be rewarded with revenue along the way. And it's critical that everyone in the business understands that relationship, and the purpose of SEO, to really make the magic happen.

Applying these sorts of skills, we were able to take Parkers from 300,000 unique visits per month to 1.5 million in 2009. Eventually, I was approached by the people who ran Honest John, who asked if I'd like to join as editor, build a team and try to achieve similar results for them.

## Using data-driven content to find your audience

At Honest John, we took the opportunity to try out things that none of our rivals were pursuing at that point. We pioneered opening up big datasets to turn them into something that grabbed the consumer's attention, giving them new and meaningful analysis. Generally these were government datasets that were, on paper, open, and anyone could use them, but few people knew how. In reality, the data was so difficult to process that most people wouldn't even try.

We started with the entire MoT-test dataset in 2012 – some 300 million records detailing every single MOT that had been carried out in the previous 12 months – to find trends. Things like which models had done well that year, which hadn't, and digging into parts of the country to where there were differing MOT pass rates.This was about six months' work from start to finish, but is still the biggest success I've ever had. The story was picked up by BBC Breakfast, every national newspaper, and myself and the team were on more than 40 radio stations that day.

Though painstaking at first, over the years, we developed a close way of working between SEO, editorial, data analysis and developers, so we had a good understanding of how to open up these datasets – and really knew how to capitalise on them. We showed that developing innovative content, which really strikes a chord with consumers, is the way to achieve that all-important PR and resulting website traffic. People talk about backlink building – but when you've got a really good story – you don't always need to worry about that.

With this approach, you can get the backlinks and brand mentions, and you also have a huge amount of interesting content for users. In this case, it created lots of pages for display revenue, as well. We also showed the value of getting as many of your team as possible invested in the SEO journey – and that effort helped us pick up the skills that we needed from across the business.

We then turned our minds to car-crime statistics, building a crime hotspot map with Freedom of Information request data from every UK police force. Next, using government data, we opened up a database of the types of cars that are currently on UK roads to create a 'how many exist?' feature. You could not only see how many old cars were still out there, but also how quickly the numbers were falling. We spun this as a 'my dad had one of those' story and, like the World Wildlife Fund does for endangered animals, we talked about 'endangered cars'.

Again, that brought in the backlinks and another stint on BBC Breakfast, but most importantly, it was shared among people themselves, as lots of people had fond car memories. It even grew a cult following among car enthusiasts. The story had arms, legs and wheels of its own, getting shared by the motoring community and bringing in new, unique users, without us pulling it along through backlinks or tailored SEO.

# Getting ahead of the keywords

A lot of SEOs just look at keyword volumes, yet they don't necessarily understand the subject that they're talking about, or the intent that is behind those volumes. In automotive, there's all kinds of intent, from buying, owning or running a car, to fans of particular makes. If you can connect with a large number of readers and have some insight into their concerns and habits, you get all kinds of insights that don't come up in keyword-volume searches. You can even get there before it's picked up through keyword searches and cement yourself as the authority ahead of everyone else. You have to turn investigator sometimes, and that is where I always return to my roots in journalism.

One example of this is something we did at Honest John about 10 years ago. We were getting huge amounts of information from our readers that indicated that car manufacturers weren't being truthful about fuel-consumption figures. So we set up a service, called Real MPG (Miles Per Gallon), where we crowdsourced fuel-consumption data. It became a runaway success, one of the most successful parts of the site, and this was all before the emissions scandal of 2015.

Once that kicked off, we were positioned as the experts, because we'd been talking about it for years and we already ranked well for the subject matter. The data even ended up being used in European Commission reports, which meant great backlinks and great PR. But the reason we'd been talking about it for years was because that's what our readers had been telling us. That's what was troubling people. So we were offering a service that people actually wanted, and that information wasn't really coming up in keyword searches anywhere else.

We took Honest John from around 350,000 or 400,000 unique visits to nearly 3 million per month by 2017. There was some CRM and brand activity, but that growth was nearly all search led. A big part of the reason heycar acquired Honest John was they'd seen what the editorial team had done and wanted us to do that for heycar as well. The website's success led to my own success too, on a personal level, I'd started out as editor and built an incredible team, by the time I left I had been promoted to editorial director and had a seat on the board.

heycar actually comprises five UK websites – including heycar and Honest John – but there's also three websites that were acquired recently that don't yet have content propositions. This gives us the option of doing some very interesting things from a content and SEO point of view, to get wide reach and tailor each offer to a specific market.

One of the greatest challenges that we've faced over the last couple of years has been building our reputation from scratch, in order to get publications to consider us as a credible voice in the automotive market and so come to us for comment. This is the cornerstone of our backlink building strategy, and has required a huge amount of time, investment and expectations management. But that's paying off – we're now seeing links coming in regularly from authoritative sites and an increase in organic links.

We've come a long way in a short amount of time – and we've thankfully had noticeable support from our CEO, CMO and the entire leadership team. We're fortunate that they get SEO and why it's critical to the company's future. This kind of buy-in is vital if you want to get projects, which won't start to pay-off for up to two years, pushed through against competing non-SEO priorities that may see faster results.

I'm very intrigued about what's happening with Expertise, Authority, Trust (EAT) over the next couple of years, because Google has been signalling recently that this is going to play an ever-bigger role in how it ranks websites. From my perspective, it will completely justify our approach of building our expertise through a content-led SEO strategy.

# How to build, execute and measure your SEO strategy

## LIDIA INFANTE
### SENIOR SEO MANAGER, SANITY.IO

After her first marketing job moved to Ibiza without her, Lidia went into ecommerce PPC. Using some of what she what she was learning here, including knowing what women were searching for, and that useful information was limited, she set up a feminist magazine. This was wildly successful, going from nothing to 750,000 organic sessions a month within a year. It caught the eye of the magazines director at RBA, the biggest magazine publisher in Spain, and she was invited to be the digital editor-in-chief for its wellness brands. She's now in the UK focusing on SEO for SaaS, mentors other women in SEO and has just released a study on inequality in SEO article authorship.

My day-to-day is making business cases, managing agencies and managing stakeholders, essentially, which I think is the case for most people who are in-house and part of a big corporation. We're about 2,000 employees. There's a lot less execution, and a lot more direction setting, getting people bought in and maintaining that direction. I think that's one of the biggest challenges as an in-house SEO – because a VP will agree to something one month – then have absolutely completely forgotten about it. It takes a lot of skill, and communication skills, to maintain your direction, and to make sure that your lovely strategy's not just a strategy – that it goes all the way to execution. And then you measure it and go back to all of your stakeholders to say, 'hey, thank you for signing off on those things, look at the revenue result'. And then they should like you more and will give you more money to do more things.

The very, very first thing that I did when I joined Sanity.io was get an understanding of what had been done before, who the stakeholders are, and have conversations with each one to understand how my work impacts their objectives. Because then I can talk to them in a language that matters to them. So if an objective is Marketing Qualified Leads (MQLs), I'm going to talk MQLs to this person. If it's cost-per-acquisition (CPA) reduction, I'm going to talk in terms of how much we're saving by putting more money into SEO. If we're talking conversion, retention, revenue, you need to understand the way your stakeholder is thinking of you as a resource.

Then you have to start looking at how you're performing and, essentially, the very first thing you need to know to grow your SEO is to understand that you are not ranking in a vacuum. You are trying to be better than the rest of your competitors. There are 10 slots on the first search results page, and you need to be in the top 10 of everyone who's trying to rank for that keyword. And in order for you to rank, you need to understand what the others are doing. Otherwise, you cannot know if you're better or worse. This is something that I do using the 'SEO gap methodology', which brings it back to the fact that we are ordering websites in terms of quality.

The three pillars of SEO are technical, content and links, and this is how we structure the gap analysis, because it's the most universal way to actually talk about SEO. And it's going to serve most websites. But the very first thing you want to do is identify your competitors, which means they have to meet three criteria – they're talking to the same audience, they are ranking for your target keywords and they're trying to solve the same problem or satisfy the same need that you're trying to satisfy. So they are effectively making you unnecessary, if your audience chooses to go with them. There are different frameworks you can use to look at it. But these are going to be the people that show up in the SERPs, as well as you, and the people who are also product competitors.

## Understanding content

In terms of benchmarking content, you can look at how much, how often, they're publishing. You can look at how much traffic they get for every editorial URL. Then there is a metric I call 'editorial efficiency', and it tells me how good a competitor is at actually targeting the search market – including the number of keywords they are ranking for in positions one to 30.

Something I find super useful is dividing the estimated traffic into branded traffic, product traffic and editorial traffic. I love using Semrush for this as it gives you a very easy way to split estimated traffic into these categories. And you don't have to download anything or use formulas. What I'm trying to understand is whether these competitors have a lot of brand awareness amongst my target audience, are people specifically searching for them? I want to see what type of questions my competitor is trying to answer in their editorial content and how they've determined the audience's interest.

So, for example, if I'm talking about 'ecommerce', I'm also probably going to be talking about 'marketing', 'online marketing', 'social media', 'TikTok selling', 'how to build a following'. I'm also going to be talking about 'CRM', 'analytics'. And 'logistics'. If I hadn't actually researched what my competitors talk about and I'm new in this industry, it will take much longer and many conversations internally to understand, 'what are we talking about?'.

Then the product traffic is going to tell me – how likely am I to actually be selling? How likely am I to be ranking for bottom-of-the-funnel queries? And it will also inform me about how many bottom-of-the-funnel queries there are in my market. Because if you're in SaaS, they're much more scarce than if you're in fast fashion – people searching 'ecommerce CMS' is a fraction of people looking for 'jeans'.

Then we're onto brand metrics. So I would measure domain authority, which is a nice guideline for a combination between the amount and quality of the links my competitors have. It's not a ranking factor. And it's not very accurate. But it's a good indicator of the link quality of my competitors.

## Finding links

Then I do something called a 'link gap analysis', where I measure the number of referring domains and total backlinks that each of my competitors have. And I measure the difference against myself. Do I have more or less referring domains? Are my competitors always getting backlinks from the same publisher and is that the reason they have so many?

And then I look at link growth, to understand whether or not they are actively link-building or doing digital PR. So I measure the number of links they had 12 or six months ago, depending on how fast the market is moving. Then I measure how many they have now and the percentage difference. From that I can tell you if they're aggressively link-building. Because even if I come out on top, if they're being very aggressive, I need to keep a very close eye on this, to make sure that I stay as the leader.

I also look at brand search volume, which is different from branded traffic, and this is going to tell me how popular this brand is on its own, how many people are searching for it. It's a good indicator of brand awareness, without having to pay for special types of market research. And then I look at brand positioning – how they're describing themselves on their homepage title, meta title and headings. This is qualitative, but it's going to give me an idea of how each of these brands is presenting its value.

## Getting technical

Technical SEO is really difficult to measure. But I've tried different things and settled for a type of measure, based on web-performance optimisation measurements. So I'd be using PageSpeed Insights, or Lighthouse scores, on mobile and on desktop, to understand how optimised the competitors' pages are for speed.

Then I'm going to be looking at the Core Web Vitals scores, so I grab the main three Core Web Vitals signals and I use the Chrome UX report, which is public on Google Data Studio. From there, I just grab the number of URLs that are qualifying as 'good' and give an average for each of the Core Web Vitals. And that's a perfectly good metric to be looking at.

Once we've identified competitors, and we've benchmarked, we're now going to find our focus. So, we'll look at the wider gap analysis and essentially identify 'this is where I'm weakest' and decide to focus on that first. But also use your internal knowledge here because, if you're more or less equally weak at content and tech, but you know that your company cannot impact tech easily, you should lean onto content, because that's what's going to give your results. And, say we identify that content is our weakest spot, we can then dive deeper into the metrics that we've used for the gap analysis. We'd be looking at ranking keywords, content-production velocity and editorial efficiency, and we're going to try to make a roadmap to meet our highest competitor. So, if they're doing 20 new pieces of content per month, and we're only doing five, we'll be looking to up it.

At this point, we're creating a roadmap of how we're going to improve amongst our competitors. It's going to be different in every gap analysis, for every company. So it comes down to best judgement. If your content is not high-quality enough, and you're not getting as many visits, why is that? Maybe you need to work on your expertise, authoritativeness and trustworthiness (EAT). Maybe your content is not comprehensive enough. This is the work that you do at this stage.

## Selling top down or bottom up?

And – this is relevant for in-house SEOs specially – you need to create that roadmap with dates, responsibilities, deliverables and expected revenue impact, and sell it to your stakeholders. Many people do the 'stakeholder sell' in many different ways. Some people like to go for the highest person and then trickle it down with the approval of the highest stakeholder. Some people share it with minor stakeholders and then it comes to the highest stakeholder with all of the support from the bottom up.

When you're doing a top-down approach, it's less comprehensive and less sustainable, but more effective. So if you're trying to get something done urgently, it's probably the best approach. If you're trying to build stakeholder relationships, it's better if you bring it to the stakeholders and then take it to the top. When you're doing top-down approaches, the CMO is not going to bring up concerns about the messaging of X thing or other things that your stakeholders are going to care about. And you're putting the pressure on them to accept something that they might not be 100% on board with. It gets it done faster. But it is not a good long-term approach.

With costings, dates, deliverables, and revenue impact off the back of that – you should find an easy 'yes'. And then you make sure that you execute by looping in project management, anyone that's actually working on the execution. And then after three months, or six months, or 12 months, depending on how you're working, you measure how much you've closed the gap.

I have developed the methodology over the last couple of years and when I'm doing mentorship for women in tech, I always share it. I also always talk to them about closing the wage gap, not only the SEO gap, because you can use and leverage this information, how you've made the company grow, how you've made the company money, to get a promotion or get paid more. Scientific studies prove that women are less likely to self promote and shout about their achievements. So the best thing that you as a woman can do in SEO, right now for equality, is go get your promotion, go get your pay rates, based on the evidence of the work you do, go get the power to then bring up other women with you.

# Leading organic growth in a business with transformational growth ambitions

## MATT JOHNSON

**SENIOR GROWTH MARKETING MANAGER, GOCARDLESS**

---

Matt started building his SEO skills at home while studying for a Marketing degree at university. After securing some freelance work during this time, his first full-time role was leading marketing for a private health-insurance broker. He then went into an SEO executive job at Photobox, then joined Dixons Carphone where he led SEO across its electronics brands. Keen to work in an agile technology firm, he joined GoCardless in 2019 to set up the SEO team here.

---

Setting something up from zero really appealed to me – building things in the way I think they should be built. GoCardless seemed like a highly agile company where we could move quickly. In these environments, you can break things, learn quickly and improve. When I joined, there was a lot of excitement about the potential for, and expectation from, SEO to become a core growth lever, at least at the leadership level. And there was a real desire to move on from a reliance on paid spend, which would make our approach to marketing much more sustainable. So the first objective was to try to prove it could be done.

## From excitement to forming a plan

Initially, you have to find out what 'becoming a core growth lever' actually looks like. What are the wider business goals? What SEO work has already been done – and what does great look like? Because if you go into a business, and there's a lot of excitement about how SEO could be the next big channel, sometimes, the tangibles are a bit different. So it was about getting alignment and then building a plan around that – trying to understand what inputs would be needed to generate the necessary output. This can even mean asking ourselves, 'are we looking to generate top-of-funnel metrics, like sessions or visibility? Or are we trying to drive signups? Or, are we trying to drive the lower-funnel metrics, like activations and revenue?'.

Then, you need detail – what percentage of these things need to come from SEO, compared to all the other channels? What are the plans across the other channels and what activity is going on elsewhere? This is all to understand what the expectation is around what will come from SEO. Then, once you've understood the objectives, you have to decide what you'll actually do to drive that. Particularly for us, that meant finding out what the core levers might be for SEO in a fintech SaaS business. And, of course, experimenting first, then doubling-down on what works.

It was quickly apparent that the core, low-funnel, high-intent keywords that are very relevant to our value proposition, like those on direct debit topics, were fairly saturated by the business already. We had content already ranking in high positions. But there was more to be gained, so we did some optimisation around identifying the keyword gaps that we already had content for.

Then, we started on keyword research for topics that are further up the funnel – what you could consider the 'consideration' area – so looking there, prioritising, scrutinising the STAT ranking, then producing content. From a theoretical perspective, we wanted to set a hypothesis that a) people were searching for these topics, and b) if a financial brand ranks for these topics, people are open to choosing our site. Then, if we can keep them on the site, can we convince them of our value proposition? So it wasn't, 'let's see if we can rank for these keywords', it was 'can we rank, and if so, will the searcher be interested in our product offering?'.

We then did a persona-led keyword research project based on what we'd learned. In the initial stages, we weren't really interested in whether a keyword would drive a session, we asked ourselves, 'will this keyword bring someone from our target persona onto our website?'. So they could be searching for all manner of topics, as long as we captured the right kind of person, we could then introduce them to GoCardless' value proposition.

# Building the right structure

I initially managed to bargain with our Head of Content for a small number of articles a month, but to their team, it felt like a lot, as they were broadly focused on a different part of our business and targeted on multimedia campaigns. We started to get the results with this bit of resource, but if you want to scale your traffic aggressively, especially at a fairly fresh company where you're building from zero, you need to scale your content aggressively too. And when you're working with teams with different KPIs, it becomes very difficult. I set up the reporting so that we had clear visibility of our leading indicators, to show it was working, and, if you're trying to scale quickly, you really haven't got time to wait for the lagging indicators.

Next it was about trying to prove that the lagging indicators would come and the performance would continue – we just needed to invest three, or four-times more to drive this outcome. But that volume of content wouldn't be matched by an in-house team, unless we could scale that team significantly.

Instead, we decided to bring in an external agency, and the current setup is preferable for both teams. We needed a scaled-up content team to help us streamline the process as much as possible, from keyword research, to briefing, to producing, to getting content documents ready to be uploaded to the blog. And that's why we brought in support to do that.

Even while we're scaling, we're still looking at those leading indicators, trying to make sure they're the right things to look at, and that we have sensible targets based on those. And you're also taking a step back, looking to those core business objectives, too. You're really trying to understand, 'what are the mechanics right at the bottom, in the granular detail of SEO activity, that will enable us to hit those targets?'. For me, you're focused on building a 'content machine', where you can relatively confidently predict, 'if we produce this much content, we'll get this much traffic, and if we sustain the conversion rates we'll get this many signups'. Then the lower funnel metrics will follow. So, for my team, I try to reduce the noise, to just focus on those indicators and the inputs that help you move towards them.

## Making the business case for a proper SEO budget

Securing the right budget was actually quite a long process, but for me it was a rewarding experience. I think, typically there's kind of an 'accepted amount' that seems sensible for a business to spend on SEO, and it's normally benchmarked by what we're spending on other channels. That does a bit of a disservice to SEO. What we did instead was work out how to build a detailed business case for unlocking the right SEO budget, which I hadn't encountered before. So we had done our early experimentation. We'd built our 'prediction model'. Then, we built a model of the Total Addressable Market (TAM) for search, what the likely penetration of that search volume would be for us, and looked at what the required investment would be to produce the content to drive that traffic.

The other side of it was to look at the core financial metrics of the business, things like our activation rates, average revenue-per-user and payback periods. We really dug deep into those, and modelled those out based on the conversion rates of the predicted traffic. We also set three different levels of 'budget ask', and then a bracket for performance within each of those so that we could give different levels of risk appetite. Then you have a much more compelling argument, backed up by data and logic, rather than arbitrary figures. This forms a very detailed and compelling case for the long-term return-on-investment of a project. If you have all of that, it becomes a much easier request. Of course, the actual returns, the payback periods, are very long, but once you reach them, the returns are very high, from an SEO perspective.

We have revisited this work, and it's not all perfect, but it's broadly correct. There's a quote attributed to George Box which says, 'all models are wrong, but some are useful'. This one is definitely useful. While it's wrong in some ways, at least it gives you something to aim for, track against and rally behind as a team. Traffic is definitely outperforming, but from a conversion rate perspective, we've realised that we need to add complimentary activity to SEO. So we've kicked off conversion-rate optimisation projects – and we've brought that into the organic growth team as well – so now we own that metric. In most SEO teams I've been in before, we have been focused solely on building traffic to the website, but I think having a single team working on both organic traffic and conversion of that traffic generates much better quality of work. So if you have one team owning both, our goals are to drive more traffic and improve the volume of signups. And we have had a really positive impact on those metrics since we started that activity that we wouldn't have seen without kicking that off.

It was a very different approach selling the business case to our exec team and our senior leadership team, but it was a great example of building a business case and unlocking budget for SEO. I think the way that we look at growth marketing overall at GoCardless means we'll always be focused on the biggest opportunities. We look to invest in things that are predictable, have the potential to really scale and be transformational, if it doesn't tick all of these boxes it's likely to be just another distraction. That's how we approach it.

And it just so happens that SEO is a massive opportunity. If, overnight, another channel came up, we'd probably look at how we can capitalise. We're not a siloed SEO team – we're a growth-marketing team. Right now though, we're 100% confident that SEO will be a very important channel for our business for a long, long time, and we'll continue to assess where the biggest opportunities are.

# Being customer first in practice

## KELLY JOHNSTONE
### HEAD OF CONTENT, STAYSURE GROUP

---

Kelly studied biology and her first job was working for the Motor Neurone Disease (MND) Association, where she was simplifying research findings for those with, or affected by, the disease. Here, she found out the basics of SEO, and although her first boss suggested her spelling and grammar was lacking, she's since thrived in the world of marketing. At Staysure Group for four years, she now manages content for three travel insurance brands and a pet insurance brand.

---

When you're working in a business, you often automatically have a 'business mindset'. Being 'business-first' means that you're making decisions to help the business grow and to make more money. When it comes to content, it's tempting to say things like, 'we can give you this' or 'our services are great for this', leading with features, rather than benefits. When actually – what's a customer getting from that? If you're saying, 'we can give you a mobile phone', really, from a customer's view, you should be letting them know that you can use it to stay in contact with people. It's about not using the 'we' statements – showing how it's actually going to make their life better – is the true value of your product.

On a website page, it's about thinking about the most valuable thing to a customer when they're there. What questions do they have that we can answer, in the right format for them, that get to the point really quickly? From your point of view, you might say 'I want to add on this USP'. But actually stripping it back – and deciding what's going to help a customer make that decision – really helps to refine your content.

On the other side of it – where business-first might be about deciding that you're going to make more money – being customer-first is understanding that giving value to your customers is valuable. And that's really uncomfortable, I think, for quite a lot of businesses. Even though money is a byproduct of that. And if you're really successful, you will make more money than you will with a business-centric model.

## Putting customers first in practice

When I first started at Staysure, about four years ago, we had around 1,400 blog posts, including pancake recipes and all sorts. And we're a travel insurance brand. We had a lot of irrelevant content in there. And having irrelevant content is not customer-first. So I pulled that number down from 1,400 to about 260. A massive decrease. And that was uncomfortable for the business, because I said, 'we're going to lose 25% of our blog traffic'.

But then I explained the 'why' – that because we were thinking customer-first – we were getting rid of all of these irrelevant blogs. Yes, some were performing well in the SERPs, but we had to ask, 'well, is that helping my relevance there? Is it helping a customer to trust us a little bit more with their product?'. So it's about having the strength to get rid of content that isn't performing as well, or that might look like it's performing, but isn't helping your brand.

I also proved that the blogs we were removing weren't helping us with any conversions. I looked at conversion-attribution modelling for all of those blogs that were bringing in traffic – and none of them were helping us drive conversions. This meant shifting away from the 'funnel model', which I dislike, because that just forces people to push more traffic in the top so that we get more people in the bottom. Instead, I was pushing the 'flywheel model', which was created by HubSpot a few years ago, and pushes the value method. So you say, 'what pain points can we focus on from a customer point of view?'.

From a customer's point of view, looking at a blog – you're almost never expecting it to convert – so you should never look at a conversion rate on a site-wide level. If you're pulling in pages that are never going to convert, why would you measure them in that way? Of course, I could delete all the content on the blog and say, 'look, I've doubled the conversion rate', because then I'm only looking at my commercial pages.

Also, looking at conversion rates on a site-wide basis is never a good way of measuring things, because, where I've taken out all of that traffic, it actually automatically increased my conversion rate. But has that actually increased my conversions? No. If someone's just driven by one metric like this, rather than looking at it from a customer's point of view, then you're not going to get a clear picture. That's why, when we're looking at our content as a team, we always push the conversation out to ask what the intent of the pages are.

A great example of this is when easyJet, a couple of years ago, saw their site traffic go through the roof. In fact, their sites crashed, because, during the pandemic, lots of people were going into their customer services section. So traffic doesn't always mean more transactions. It's about making sure that you can bucket that customer intent, to make sure that you're reporting on those different problems and scenarios in a way that makes sense, rather than just, from a business point of view, saying 'we have more traffic, that must mean we're making more money'.

Of course, some blog pages do convert, if they are lower down towards someone's intent to buy. So, for example, in my industry, it's things like 'should I buy travel insurance if I have a heart murmur?'. This is an example of a more informational-intent question, but they're thinking about buying anyway. So this will be more of an FAQ-style blog. It would obviously be boring if we emailed our customers with information just about travel insurance all the time, because most people won't need to buy travel insurance if they've just bought their cover, or don't have a trip lined up yet. But a blog about a holiday, for example, travel tips – someone's not thinking about buying their travel insurance – yet. They're getting inspiration for going on holiday which they may later need to cover. But, being able to increase someone's trust over time with a relevant blog means they can then move down towards converting.

I would never get my team to write an article purely for SEO, though. I think that's a wrong concept, too. Because, if you're writing an article 'for search', you'll be missing a trick, if you're not also factoring in things like social, email and all the other channels where you can use that content. If you're just writing it for one purpose and not repurposing, centralising content in your business, then you're missing out on opportunities.

I manage the social team at Staysure Group too and we have relationships with the email team, so our centralised content planner feeds into their email schedule, as well as feeding into social. An article will probably be the central part of what we do, but then we might get an influencer to talk about that topic on one of our social-media channels. And then we'll mention it in an email to push traffic to that blog page, or wherever we're producing content. I think that's one of the interesting things with content, it's not just your web content, it's wherever people are consuming. And wherever people have communities around your topics.

Two of the travel brands I manage – one for over 50s and one for over 70s, are ranked on page one for 'travel insurance' – but it can be difficult, managing two brands that have a similar target. It's about making sure, from a content strategy point of view, that they fulfil different needs, that you aren't just going for 'tips for Spain' for both. And if something like that is a really important search term for both, it's about making sure that we're dealing with those in a way that's relevant for different demographics, making sure that we understand that it's a different sort of customer.

Although it's been a really difficult period for the travel industry, the company decided not to let anyone go during the COVID-19 pandemic. I actually went from managing one person to managing eight through that period. Now we're coming out the end of that – we have big ambitions – and the biggest problems we face now, as ever, is resource.

# Is your marketing ageist?

We have two brands in travel insurance – Staysure and Avanti – one that's meant to be aimed at the over-70s and one aimed at the over-50s, both medical. And one of my biggest frustrations is that tools like Google Analytics only measure in any detail up to age 65.

Everyone else gets put into age brackets, part of the Google profile, based on their interests and things, to roughly guess how old people are in your Analytics account. It goes up roughly in five to 10-year age gaps. And then 65-plus is just 65-plus, that's it. We still find people in their 80s who are tech savvy, but for the vast majority of our traffic, we can't actually look at profiling information, we can't target them or measure that – you no longer matter in terms of analytics, at least from a visit perspective. I think they're missing a trick.

It might be because there aren't many brands that actively focus on people over 65. And when you think about people in their 60s, you might think about something like Stannah stairlifts, which aren't the sexiest of products in the world. A lot of these brands don't seem to focus on being customer-first, because it's like, 'oh, well, these people don't matter anyway'. It feels like you get a lesser customer experience – and they're really forgotten, in terms of advertising too – even though they're children of the 60s, so it's most likely they do not have an innocent past. They're not all frumpy.

Quite a lot of people that start with us assume 'we have to talk to this person in a very formal way'. But you can talk conversationally with someone in their 60s. I think it's really important, if you're working for a different demographic, to actually talk to them, and understand how they think, how they feel, rather than making assumptions. As part of our onboarding process, we spend a lot of time with our customer services and our sales team to listen to their calls, and see what sort of questions they have. I think that's probably something that's missed in other businesses.

If someone is older, they're more likely to want to call us, really because, if they have a long list of medical conditions, it may be easier. Though they are tech savvy, and they found us online, they just want to talk to someone just to make sure that they've got everything covered. A younger demographic doesn't usually behave in the same way – because they don't have as many medical conditions, they're happier to do that online – and they generally don't want to talk to people.

# Having brave conversations can improve the user experience for everyone

## RYAN JONES
### SEO SPECIALIST, LAND OF RUGS

---

Ryan started his digital career as a 16-year-old apprentice at an agency in Derby – getting experience in everything from search to social. After finishing his qualification, he'd fallen in love with SEO and soon landed an in-house role at an IT firm. Now he's leading on SEO for a family-run business, Land of Rugs, and he's got his own apprentice marketer.

---

When it comes to SEO, for me, forget backlinks, forget content, forget your tech stack and everything else, if people are having a crappy experience on your site, then you're not going to get very far.

You can spend as much time and as much money as you want, and put all this amazing content out there for all to see. You can have links from all these high-authority sites that get you loads of traffic, but it's not going to help if people come to your site, have a bad experience, and then bounce and go to a competitor. If the traffic bounces, what's the point? I don't think that you can do any good with SEO if you don't have a good user experience.

## A brave conversation

At Land of Rugs last year, we got hit by one of Google's infamous updates and, essentially, we lost 30% of the traffic to our site in about three days. Being an ecommerce business, that was pretty shocking. It obviously had impacts on revenue and everything like that. Naturally, I was kind of worried for my job and for the business as well.

There was quite a broad spectrum of things I could do next – but one of the key things – was going to the director and saying, 'look, I want to completely delete 70% of the blog'. This naturally got a little bit of pushback. I'd only really been in the business for about six or seven months.

But a lot of the content on the blog was really thin, less than 100 words, and it might have this amazing title that draws you in, '10 ways to make your living room feel bigger', which sounds great as a user until they land on the page and realise there is no detail.

If you were to sit and read a lot of the blogs, from a user's perspective, it just wasn't helpful content. And none of it was ranking, so it was useless content on the site anyway.

The biggest thing that helped me make my case was finding examples of where other websites that had content that had hindered performance, and how they'd reformed the content on their site, helping bring the site back and even improve it from where they were.

One of the other big things was to try to get the data to tell a bit of a story – to try to make the data really, really easy to understand and explainable. Rather than just saying – 'we need to change these internal links, they're probably a contributing factor to the fact that nobody who lands on this page buys' – pointing them to cold, hard numbers, and showing how the changes you make improve business metrics, like revenue and conversion rate, rather than just traffic and bounce rates.

I definitely think it's healthy to disagree with your boss sometimes. If you can disagree, in a healthy way, and say, 'let's find some data and see who's right', then you can drive really good business impact. It helped that my boss understood that in this case, it was just a Google update, he knew it's not anything that we'd done to the site. I think the key is to sit down and have a good discussion, and use data to really try and help you make your point, rather than just going in with a gut feeling.

You can admit that you don't have data and say, 'well, let me have half an hour, I'll go and find you some'. Another big thing is admitting if you are wrong as well; if you have a good idea, and then you can't find the data to support it, then go back to them and admit that.

## A good experience

So luckily, I managed to get buy-in for deleting and rewriting a lot of the blog, as well as reforming all the category pages on the website. It was a massive amount of work and we put a massive amount of budget into it, including my time and development time, to revamp the whole site, to make the user experience better.

And we're now at a stage where we're ranking better than we ever have before, and beating some of the top competitors in the space, even though we definitely don't have as many backlinks as they do. The goal with the new blog was, even if you come in at the very start of your buying journey, maybe you're just looking for ways to make your living room a little bit more minimalist, then we can help you.

Now we have content that's really long-form – posts that will take you 15 or 20 minutes to read in full – into things like different design elements like, 'Scandi', 'boho' and all things like this. If we help you, hopefully you'll come back and buy a rug from us when you're ready to actually buy.

We can see in the data that users are having a good experience. They're coming onto the blogs, and actually sitting and reading them, which is the main thing. They're spending good numbers of minutes reading, then clicking through to other pages as well. So it shows that the work we've done has had a great impact on the site.

A lot of the smaller-scale stuff I do comes from testing out on small areas of the site. We have a great tool called SEO Testing, which doesn't cost a lot, even for a small business. It's definitely justifiable. It allows us to run really small-scale tests at first, which don't cost a lot of time and budget, and it's definitely easier to convince your boss to make changes to maybe five or six pages, rather than site-wide changes. Obviously, if those tests are successful, then you get the authority straightaway to push it through to the site.

I used this when we were deciding whether to touch the category pages after the Google update hit our traffic. They're a massive part of our site because they bring through the traffic that usually converts, rather than the blog. So I managed to convince them just to let me test on five of the less important category pages and completely rewrite the content to see what actually happens in terms of user experience. Did people stay longer on the site? Do they click through to more pages? It was a pretty successful test, we got a more than 50% uplift in the traffic to those pages. Users were all staying longer on the site, clicking through to filters, and actually buying more. We could see that in the data then, so we got buy-in from that point to push that out.

Google updates do still blindside people, in the sense that they don't tend to announce what they're doing until they're actually starting the rollout. But there are people you can follow on Twitter, who monitor changes in the results pages, and can sometimes point to an update happening in the very near future, so you can prepare yourself. But it's worth remembering – this really is just Google trying to make the results pages better for the user – which is why focussing on user experience is definitely going to be your best bet.

## Passing the baton

As someone who came into SEO as an apprentice, I would definitely like to see apprenticeships become more mainstream. I think it's potentially one of the best learning tools that young people have, if they want to get into marketing, because they can experience how a business works, whether that's an agency or in-house.

The key thing I always say is to try to build relationships with people, even if they're not in your work network – connect with people on Twitter, LinkedIn, join communities like Traffic Think Tank. So you can really drill down deep with people who have been in the industry for longer than you have. Because there may come a time, like I am now, where you're the person who is responsible for SEO for a million-pound business. So really try to form connections with people that might be able to help you.

There can be a lot of office politics, and moments where you need to have brave conversations, if you want to get into leadership positions, so you definitely have to get to understand how office politics work. And you won't get a better sense of that than when you're working in the office.

# Voice SEO is dead - long live visual SEO.

## ANTONIS KONSTANTINIDIS
### SENIOR SEO MANAGER, CHARLOTTE TILBURY

---

Antonis got a taste of SEO when he started working at Betfair in 2006, where he was asked to optimise its Greek sports pages, and made it the number-one international blog for the sports betting brand. After a number of SEO roles in sports marketing, fintech and education, he joined luxury beauty brand Charlotte Tilbury in 2021.

---

My first taste of SEO was more than 10 years ago – when I was at Betfair. I worked as a general, digital sports marketing executive, but I was given the task of helping on the Greek blog, and optimising it. It was something no one was really interested in, but I started working on it, and had really great success.

It was then I realised that, by writing good articles, you can start to get a lot of traffic from Google organic search. The blog was the number-one international blog for the company, bringing a lot of organic traffic and revenue to my department. This was the start of my initial interest to understand why and how Google works. This was about luck – but also a clear interest in determining how things work.

My first real SEO role came again, by accident, because I was working at a company called Smart Live casino and unfortunately, I lost my job. As it happened, PokerStars were looking for a Greek SEO manager, so I went for the interview and they really never believed that they could find an SEO specialist from Greece. Just by showing my interest in SEO, and the bit of experience I had, I got the position, and that was more or less how it all started.

## Understanding intent

It's really important to fully understand the intent of people who use search, and that was really the first thing I learned at Betfair. I didn't really know 'how I should optimise for them –I just knew that my customers would be interested in sports, or horse racing or casinos. That also meant knowing that 'horse racing' does not really translate exactly in Greek.

Today at Charlotte Tilbury, it's not simply writing about 'makeup', in our case, but 'what's the best makeup style for a Saturday night?'. That is the difference between writing an article and writing an article that satisfies the user intent. I was always looking to come into the beauty industry – I think the main reason was because it is really, really competitive, in terms of SEO, but also in terms of any digital marketing channel. So I really liked the opportunity to, let's say, compete, and try to achieve results.

That's one of the great things when you work in SEO. As long as you understand the techniques, as long as you understand the reasoning behind SEO, I think you can apply that to any industry. SEO has evolved, but as long as you put the user at the forefront, and don't compete against Google, you are going to be alright.

Obviously, the product is different, but there aren't many differences working as an SEO manager at Charlotte Tilbury compared to a gaming company. Maybe the main one is that 10 years ago our SEO team was mainly male-dominated, while today I am working together with highly talented female SEOs, something that is great for our industry. But even if the people look different – the dynamic and the way they're structured have a lot of similarities – they're both really fast paced and competitive. I could probably find more differences between education and maybe fintech, than beauty and gaming.

## Getting started in beauty SEO

I think we do understand the value of SEO at Charlotte Tilbury, and what it brings to the company, and they were ready to make changes, which is not always the case. Like every company, there is always a struggle to understand how we can put a monetary value on any changes you want to bring, and I think it's always a matter of how we can take it even further.

Really, we are a tech company and so a lot of our day-to-day work has to do with optimising our website technically. We're an international brand focusing on eight different markets and the company is expanding all the time. Right now we're building new websites that focus on additional markets and sending products all over the world.

We have two main product categories – makeup and skincare – and day-to-day my focus is monitoring all those relevant keywords for my industry. I have gathered all those keywords and chucked them on a big SEO tool and we are monitoring their performance every week.

Probably the biggest change that we have managed so far is content optimisation on our website. We started working mainly with our blog and really understanding how important it is to write less, rather than more, content. We are now working more on how we blend content – because sometimes brands have different content for users and different content targeting search engines. So we're trying to blend that content to make sure that whatever we create, it is great for social media, for CRM, for search engines too.

One of the things that we do, as a department, is help other teams understand how we can help them shape new products. Internally, we build products, and SEO can help, by delivering information about users. We can tell them what they are looking at right now and we have tools to understand the seasonality of keywords – how users are searching different keywords in January, versus December, or in June in the UK, versus Australia, and this can be really, really different in every country.

But it's also about platforms. One of the things I'm trying to push people to understand is how the platforms change. We might think that search is all about Google, that's the first thing that comes to everyone's mind when they talk about SEO, but people are searching on YouTube, on TikTok, on Maps, people are searching everywhere.

## Exploring visual search

Generally, there is always the question 'what is the next Google and how will people continue searching?'. A couple of years ago 'voice search' came onto the scene and everybody said that we will use our mobiles, or voice assistants, like Amazon Echo, to search. I didn't quite believe the hype – and I think I've been correct on that. Maybe that will change in the next few years. I'm 40 years old, so maybe the newer generation might search differently. Never say never.

My experience is that, if you understand how SEO works, and you're already working in search, there are very few things that you can do on top of that to rank on voice search. Essentially, it's not something new.

99

As long as you're ranking number-one on desktop, or on mobile, there is a pretty high percentage, 95% to 99%, that you also rank high in voice search.

However, where I think that there is an additional opportunity, where you need to do many more things in order to rank, is visual search. By visual search I mean, in essence – images and video. Alongside Google itself, and Google image search, YouTube has for some time been one of the most-searched places in the world. A lot of users check it for reviews before they buy a product, so there's a lot of possibilities for marketers.

To rank in visual search, it's important to know that you need to do many more things that marketers do not necessarily do right now. You need to create content that is visual, either images, or videos, and optimise your website for that.

There are brands testing it – Tommy Hilfiger, during a runway show, had the models going up and down – and everybody was taking pictures with the app from Tommy Hilfiger. They could see at that point, what every model was wearing, and how much it cost and they were driving traffic from the show directly to their website, and they were converting new customers.

When you go to ASOS, you have the ability to 'check your style', and you can upload a picture, or put in your own preferences, and then ASOS will come back with results about the best clothes for you. In order to do that, they need to have optimised the website in such a way that it can crawl and analyse all the images they have and categorise them, and bring relevant results back to the user.

Coinbase had a really simple ad with a QR code on it during the latest Super Bowl, where users could scan that QR code on the TV and they were transferred to the website, which eventually crashed. Obviously, that was huge PR for them. I'm wondering how we take that and we transfer it more to our industry and our channel.

# SATISFYING INTENT

At Charlotte Tilbury, we have what we call a 'virtual store' and here the company is now exploring its position in the 'metaverse'. The question is – how do we use the metaverse, or how do we use those new technologies – for search optimisation in the next few weeks, or years? For me, if you're in the beauty industry, you need to see the product, especially online, because you're not there physically in the store to try it, so any visualisation that you have is very important.

So we can see a lot of brands already testing visual search opportunities, not everybody has got it right, but they're really, really working for that. From these cases, and tools that can show how many people are searching keywords on platforms like YouTube, we've started to get better data about how companies might profit from visual search, and how they use it to convert more people, to get more brand awareness and get bigger.

What we do know is – users will keep searching like this – so the question, as an SEO manager, is how can you be across all of those areas? Of course, it depends on your industry and it's not easy to predict what will work best, but I think you need to take time to understand – what's the company that you represent? What is your product? How will your users be searching for it? It's always about the same thing in the end – satisfying intent.

# SEO and accessibility go hand in hand

## DIANE KULSETH
### SENIOR SOLUTION EXPERT, SEO, SITEIMPROVE

---

SEO was recommended to Diane by one of her mentors at college, who recognised that she had both editorial and technical skill. After starting out working agency-side, she went on to manage SEO for her university – and now she's teaching digital marketing at the University of Wisconsin and Loyola University New Orleans. At software product Siteimprove for more than four years, she now works closely with the company's accessibility team, to ensure companies thinking about SEO are thinking accessibility, and vice versa.

---

The biggest thing about accessibility that people don't understand is, they automatically think this is for people that are blind, or people that can't hear or they think of the wheelchair sign at a public venue where they need to have a ramp to allow someone to access a venue. It goes beyond that.

This can be people who are dealing with carpal tunnel and they can't use their dominant hand. This can be people who are dyslexic and can't read words the way that most others can. This is people who are recovering from any sort of cognitive issue, or have a cognitive issue, so people recovering from a concussion or those who have long COVID, who are dealing with brain fog. Whether it's a grandparent that has tremors in their hand, or it's you when you have an off day, there's so many different ways that accessibility is important.

And that's the thing that a lot of marketing leaders don't understand – it really literally affects everyone – it's not ok to just say, 'oh well, our product isn't for people that are blind', or 'our product isn't for people that can't hear'. Your website is for everyone, and everyone will have some sort of need for accessibility in their lifetime.

## Getting started

What I like to tell people is – it's not rocket science. It's not something where you need to get a bunch of additional tools. Very much like SEO, it's all based on standard web practices. The easiest time to make those changes is during the actual creation of a new website, or when you're refreshing a website, but even if you aren't planning an overhaul, it's something that marketers of any skill level should be able to pick up.

There are a lot of free resources where you can learn at least the basic principles of website accessibility, and there are a lot of free tools that will take a look at the accessibility of your website, at least at a high level. So then you can identify some of those initial, most critical issues, before you make an investment in a tool or an agency or some of those areas that will take you a little bit further in the execution.

At a basic level, it's about having headings in a logical order, and when you have images, making sure that you have text descriptions to describe what that image is. It's the same thing with videos, make sure you have descriptions there. If you have different HTML elements, make sure you're actually identifying, you know, 'this label pertains to a table' versus 'this pertains to a bulleted list'. It's just about providing additional clarity about the elements on your website, which shouldn't be too difficult with modern-day content management systems.

## Remember THAT when thinking SEO or accessibility

For me, there's four main areas of overlap when it comes to accessibility and SEO – and I like to use the acronym THAT: Titles, Headings, Alt text and link Text. So, when you're looking at your titles, SEOs love to talk about titles that you want to have – to make sure their keywords are in place. And you absolutely want to do that. But you also want to make sure that it's written in a great way for a web visitor to see, if they've got multiple tabs open on your website, that they can easily determine what each page is for.

For example, you might have your 'About Us' page, a shopping page, a 'Contact Us' page, and making sure those keywords are coming first and foremost helps a screen reader, or another assistive technology, to be able to discern, 'okay, this is the shopping page'. So there's nothing in conflict with SEO there, that's what SEOs are trying to do. They're trying to keep what's most important towards the front of those titles. And you don't want to have, you know, four pages that say 'Blue Array services', 'Blue Array services', 'Blue Array services', because that doesn't provide differentiation for the end user.

Headings is all about having everything in a logical order. I would often tell people, you know, go back to your secondary English class when you're writing your first papers and they would say have '123', or 'ABC', make sure you have everything in a logical order. And that's the exact same thing you want to do here. For search engines, it provides that topical relevance. For accessibility users, it provides them a quick way to be able to use their screen reader, or their other assistive technology, to quickly scan the webpage and determine where they need to go for the content they're seeking.

Considering alt text, or alt attributes, Google has recently reiterated that this is still very important for searching images, and for Google itself to be able to determine what actually is the content of those images. Same thing with screen readers and other assistive technologies, it's about being able to simply describe 'here's what's in the picture'. If you go onto Microsoft PowerPoint, or Microsoft Word, you can pop an image in and it will try to provide a description, something like 'woman smiling'. Which is like, great, that's helpful, but it's 'woman smiling while she's driving a car' that provides additional context. So being able to actually write that out in your images is not only helpful for the end user coming to the website, but also for search engines to understand what that content actually is.

And then finally, link text, or anchor text. This is, of course, important from an SEO perspective for backlinking and providing that relevance to those keywords that you're going after. For accessibility, it's important because you don't want every link to say 'read more', or 'click here' or 'submit here', you actually want to provide a little bit more of a description. So 'read more about our COVID-19 policies', or 'click here to schedule your hair appointment'. It's important to provide additional details about what people are going to see when they click.

We recently worked with a large brand that already had a great SEO team in place and they had been working really solidly on these initiatives for some time. So they decided to pivot towards accessibility and brought a couple of employees on to specifically focus on that. And, just by focusing on their web accessibility, they were able to increase the brand's overall web traffic by almost 20% year-over-year. For any marketing leader, that's something that would at least cause them to pause and say, 'okay, that's intriguing. I want to learn more about how that happened'.

As marketers, we're always talking about removing the barriers from a good conversion, being able to make sure that it's the cleanest experience, that will help users to convert to make their purchase. Accessibility is the exact same thing. You're removing those barriers that make it hard for someone to navigate your website.

## Becoming a ranking factor?

Google doesn't directly rank sites on accessibility – but the one thing that I go back to all the time is – Google is like the world's largest screen reader. And Google's mission, all search engines' missions, are to get people to the content that they want. So they are constantly looking at how information is categorised and labelled. We see this in SEO, with your structured data markup, being able to categorise different types of content. And with accessibility, it's the exact same thing, it's just labelling your content, labelling these different elements on your website.

If you go to Google's accessibility page, they talk about the fact that they want to make the web accessible to everyone. So it's one of those things where, they say accessibility isn't something that they focus on, but at the same time, they talk a lot about its importance. So today it might not directly be an algorithm factor – but it's definitely something that they're clearly aware of, and keeping an eye on.

With clients, I say, if you're looking to advance your SEO, start focusing on your web accessibility, because Google does talk about its importance, Google does talk about the need for accessibility on your websites. And they're already tracking accessibility in their Lighthouse open-source platform. So they're already monitoring 40 or so different accessibility issues. And, as someone who can be kind of sceptical, I'm like, 'why are you just tracking a bunch of different data points around accessibility on your website?'. Google doesn't track a bunch of things, just to track them. There's usually a greater purpose. For me, it's not too much of a stretch to think that it will be part of the algorithm if it's not already.

I was talking with a bunch of our accessibility leaders and I asked, 'what are the challenges that you see?' and they said, 'everyone thinks it's just a legal issue, if someone comes to our website, and they can't access it, they'll maybe submit a lawsuit, and then we'll have to deal with it'. And it's like, 'well, okay, number one, you don't want to have to wait until your company deals with a lawsuit'. But then also, everyone is going to experience some form of accessibility issue, whether it's permanent, or you're just having an off day. It's about getting beyond that whole, 'this is only for a very small portion of users', it's actually making the web easier for everyone. The more that you make your website accessible for these specific audiences, the more you make it accessible for everyone.

I would love to see the web become more passionate about diversity. And it plays well with accessibility, but it also plays into overall web performance and page speed. In 2020, we saw everyone go into their homes, whether that was for school, for work, and not everyone has the same wifi that you do in your office. Not everyone works in an office with

5G wifi, not everyone operates at 110% every single day mentally, visually, auditorily. It's just crazy to think about it like that. There's no perfect situation, where everyone has perfect internet and perfect capabilities, 24/7.

So making sure that we're optimising websites for poor connection speeds, for those that are in more rural areas, that we're taking a look at accessibility. Everyone's talking about the importance of diversity, equity and inclusion initiatives right now. And I think web accessibility and performance really play into that. You want to make sure that you provide an experience – that's an equitable experience – for everyone.

# Don't just start selling 'Lesbian Soup' – and other ways to make sure you're doing properly inclusive marketing

## SARAH MCDOWELL

### SEO MANAGER, CAPTIVATE

Sarah started her 10-year SEO career as a link builder for a digital marketing agency. Over the years, she worked her way up to become a search consultant and then project coordinator. From here, she went in-house to help sell dream holidays, then to a solicitors, had a go at freelancing, then headed back agency-side before joining the SEO team at Holland & Barrett. During the latter years of her career, Sarah started to have some tough but needed conversations about LGBTQI+ inclusivity – and she believes this can make brands, marketing – and LGBTQI+ lives – better. As well as SEO, Sarah loves podcasts and has just launched her fourth show, The SEO Mindset, so she's just landed her perfect job, as the SEO manager at Captivate, a growth-orientated podcast-hosting platform, part of the wider Global media and entertainment.

In April 2021, Kelvin, one of the organisers of brightonSEO, reached out to see if I wanted to do a talk. Very flattering. I had always wanted to speak at brightonSEO, but I didn't really know what topic to talk about. Then I realised 'hang on, I've got an opportunity here'. Inclusivity has always been a passion of mine, especially for the LGBTQI+ community, being a lesbian woman. Here I had a platform to normalise an often-taboo subject, and so the title of my talk was born, 'how to be an LGBTQI+ ally when it comes to your website, SEO and marketing'.

I understand there is nervousness around this subject, particularly about getting things wrong, and people sometimes become defensive when unintentional offence has been caused. But it's human nature to get things wrong. So this issue is really about taking accountability, having conversations to understand why offence was caused, working together to find a solution and being better in the future. It's not a case of pointing fingers at each other and saying, 'you're not doing this right, you did this wrong'. It's more about learning together, thinking how we can be better, how we can grow and develop, how we can be an ally in life, but also through our websites, marketing and SEO.

Being an ally is important. It matters. Yes, things are getting better for much of the LGBTQI+ community, though sadly not everywhere in the world, which means there's still work to be done. While doing research for my talk, I found out that every year the UK government collates hate-crime data based on lots of different criteria, including sexual orientation. According to these government stats, hate crimes based on sexual orientation are going up and up. From 2016 to 2017, to 2020 to 2021, the number has pretty much doubled to more than 17,000 reported each year.

## Opening up the conversation

After my talk at brightonSEO, I started to have more conversations about inclusivity with professionals and brands. And I've noticed there are many ways that companies can be more inclusive.

One of the most important aspects is having inclusive language and imagery on your website to avoid unintentional discrimination. For example, content teams making sure blogs use inclusive language, such as using 'parent' instead of 'mother' or 'father', or 'they' instead of 'he' and 'she'. I have also worked on inclusive website imagery, let's say you have a blog category about 'sexual health', your images shouldn't not just show hetrosexual couples. Compulsary heteorsexuality (or 'comp het', as the cool kids say) plays a big part here. This is the idea that hereorsexuality is the 'norm' and that everyone is 'straight' until they say otherwise. This is not correct and it's actually very damaging. We need to move away from this way of thinking.

You should also consider text used elsewhere on your website, such as product pages. The big question is – are you at risk of alienating anyone? Let's say you have a product to help people manage menopause symptoms. If you had text saying, 'are you a woman experiencing menopause?' this is discriminative and alientating towards people who are going through the menopause but don't identify as a woman. Switch it to say, 'are you experiencing menopause?'. Another example would be products or services for people pre-, during or post-pregnancy. Again make sure there's inclusive language, like 'parent', and 'they' and 'their', instead of 'she' and 'her'.

Pronouns are also a biggie. Don't ever assume. For example, let's say you have an 'about us' page on your website with team-member profiles. If you are writing the content, ask what people's pronouns are, don't assume what you think they should be. Normalise this conversation. I include my pronouns within my email footer and on social-media platforms. If you conduct interviews, ask the person beforehand what they prefer to be called. There was a situation with an external supplier once where I noticed you had to fill in a form to sign up to a platform and there wasn't an 'MX' gender-neutral option. I brought it to their attention and straight away they altered it. It can be that easy.

At Captivate, I'm combining my two loves, SEO and podcasting, and our main focus is helping the 'indie podcaster' be more successful by simplifying workflows and processes, growing their listenership and providing monetisation opportunities. Here, we've found an opportunity within our platform to be more inclusive and so the team is working on an update of our guest-booking tool so hosts can request a guest's pronouns so they know how to introduce them. Again normalising the conversation.

Another thing to consider is your security practices. For example, when you sign up to something online, you are sometimes asked 'what is your gender?' as a security question. That's a very personal question for some people. Some may not want to answer. If you don't need this information, don't ask. Security prompts sometimes include things like 'what is your mother's maiden name?'. But, not everyone has a mother, for example, you might have two fathers, so it's all about ensuring you give options that are accessible to everyone.

There's also your Google Business Profile (previously known as Google My Business) to consider, where you can add LGBTQI+ related attributes so people in the community know where it is safe for them to visit. Including these attributes (or if someone mentions these terms in a review they leave) means that when someone searches for something like, 'gay-friendly shops' or 'LGBT-friendly pubs', your listing will come up in the SERPs.

Of course, a big thing in SEO is keywords, so if you've got products or services for the LGBTQI+ community, you first need to find out what they're looking for, and then make sure they can find your website and pages. But only do this if you are legitimately selling a product or service for the community.

A rubbish example (but one that got a laugh during my brightonSEO talk) was that you can't go around saying you're selling 'Lesbian Soup' – we pretty much eat the same food as everyone else, would you believe. Through surveys, and getting input and feedback from the LGBTQI+

community, you can understand their needs and see if there really is a product or service you can provide that is currently not available.

# Don't jump on the bandwagon

Companies big and small have a real opportunity to do things that actually matter to the LGBTQI+ community and make a positive change. But something I don't like to see is companies jumping on the 'Pride bandwagon' every time June rolls around.

It's not good to have the mindset of, 'okay, we need a way of getting involved in Pride to sell more products – let's slap on a rainbow on a product and sell that!'. That's not what Pride is about. One major British retailer received backlash from the community when they did their take on the BLT sandwich during Pride, but added guacamole so they could call it the LGBT – and the 'Lesbian Soup' example doesn't seem so wild now. People didn't respond well, even though some money raised from selling the sandwich went to charity. Whatever the event, so-called 'slacktivism' is the practice of supporting a political or social cause by doing things that take little effort or commitment or without thinking about the impact they're having.

Similarly one of the world's biggest video platforms commissioned a Pride-themed series, which was free and accessible, so very supportive of the community. But it's also faced some criticism over the years for things like its approach to categorising LGBTIQ+ content and whether its advertising policy allows for the inclusion of anti-LGBTIQ+ brands.

Okay, now we know what not to do, let's move on to showing some good examples of companies supporting the community. One really positive example for me is the hotel and restaurant chain Kimptons. This was one of the first major hotel sponsors of the Trevor Project, which is a charity preventing suicide in LGBTQI+ youth. They have a page on their website all about LGBTQI+ inclusivity, where they talk about how they support the community, with links to LGBTQI+ related blog posts. From this, people can see that Kimptons is doing their bit to encourage positive change.

I know Starbucks gets both good and bad press. But during Pride one year they launched a really good campaign called #whatsyourname? where they partnered with Mermaids, which is a charity that supports transgender, non-binary and gender-diverse children, young people and their families. The content, social and TV campaign showed how an everyday occurrence, like ordering a coffee in a cafe, can be so big to someone who's presenting a new name for the first time.

Yes, they raised money for Mermaids, but they actually did something to get people to stop and think. To gain understanding about people going through a significant change in their life. There's a Twitter account called @dadtrans who said, 'this is a lovely, authentic story. It will mean a lot to the trans kids who see this. Thank you'.

Some people who attended my brightonSEO talk asked me, 'what if you have all the right intentions behind a campaign, but you get it wrong?'. And I know there are lots of companies that are afraid of this. One way to mitigate this is having people from within the LGBTQI+ community in your campaign team. If it's campaign about same sex-parents, for example, make sure to include them. If you can't do this, partner with a brand or charity that are experts on the subject, like Starbucks did.

Accountability matters, but we're all human, we all make mistakes. What I think is a mistake is when companies or people get on the defensive and end up digging themselves a hole when trying to find a reason to explain their behaviour, rather than putting your hands up and saying sorry.

## Recognising best practice

What I'd like to see in the future of SEO is Google and other search engines rewarding websites, brands and companies more when they focus on accessibility, diversity and inclusivity. SEO professionals and marketers only have so many hours in their working day, so if Google and search engines rewarded these aspects more when crawling websites, they would be higher up the priority list.

I also want to see more brands and organisations taking more accountability, and looking at ways they can support the LGBTQI+ community. No matter how small, it really does make a difference. No more jumping on the Pride bandwagon and rainbow washing, instead brands should be genuinely committed to supporting the community all year round. I want to see companies prioritise both accessibility and inclusivity more, rather than seeing it as a 'nice thing to have'.

We also need to normalise this conversation at home and at work. Being LGBTQI+ shouldn't be a taboo – but it may be hard to get right – and this means you need input from lots of different people and departments, including SEO, marketing, content and websites in general. More people need to know what it takes to be an ally and why it is important. It shouldn't just be left to one individual. Of course, this may be easier for bigger companies, who may have the time and money to have an internal team responsible for inclusivity, but everyone in a business can take accountability for understanding this issue more.

This way everyone, including people from the LGBTQI+ community, can feel that they matter, that brands and companies care about them and are supportive of their needs. Being inclusive is a win-win for companies, people and society. Just make sure you are doing things for the right reasons – no slapping on those rainbows – and if people can see that a business is being supportive, they are more likely to want to become your customers.

# The search for an SEO strategy for sustainable jewellery

## VIOLETTE MOUSSAVI

### SEO MANAGER, VRAI

---

Violette lives in LA and leads on SEO for the luxury, sustainable diamond brand VRAI – and it turns out that offering people an alternative like this, in a competitive search space – is a challenging task. She's focussed on SEO for the best part of a decade, and has particular expertise in sustainable brands. Violette also has her own SEO consultancy, SEOrchid

---

VRAI is a direct-to-consumer, luxury brand that started in 2014, and designs sustainable jewellery and engagement rings. The products come from our own foundry, which has zero carbon footprint, and we produce our own lab-grown diamonds.

I'm the company's first in-house SEO and that can be a fortunate position to be in – because they know that SEO is needed and you get to be the person that decides how it's done. At VRAI, SEO is the channel that brings the most revenue – so it's clear that it should be prioritised.

To me, SEO is about building a brand – it's about how you can differentiate your content from other websites. There are many other jewellery designers, but not all of them have the same sustainability practices as VRAI. It's interesting, of course, to work for a company where I can identify with their values, but this is also about finding ways to convince people to purchase from you.

## Educating the consumers

There are more and more conscientious consumers that care about the environmental impact of their purchases and so it's exciting to work for a brand that does that. But 'sustainable jewellery' itself actually doesn't have a lot of search volume. 'Lab-grown diamonds' have a lot of search volume, there are many questions people have about lab-created diamonds that create a lot of content opportunities. But not everybody knows about them.

So, in my field, a lot of content that I create is based on education – I need to educate users about lab-grown diamonds around related search queries, such as 'what are lab-grown diamonds?' or 'are lab-grown diamonds real diamonds?'. And that's what we've been focusing on, telling people that 'yes, lab-created diamonds are real diamonds' and 'it's actually better for the environment. It has no human or environmental toll'. All of this is building our topical authority, which should result in higher rankings. It's about creating the right content to educate users and increase conversions.

Diamonds are a competitive space. Often though, it's terms that are not 'on brand' for us that people are searching for. Searches for sustainable or ethical products are increasing, but it's not the majority. Which means you actually have to target users that aren't typing these search queries, but are still your target audience. So it's all about analysing the search data, and knowing the user behaviour and search trends. As our main goal is to bring more traffic, we still have to focus on broader terms, like 'diamond jewellery', that are more competitive, but at the end of the day, they're the keywords lots of people search for.

One big challenge right now is, when you're a lab-grown diamond producer, Federal Trade Commission (FTC) guidelines say that, whenever you mention the word 'diamond' on your website to describe your products, it must be accompanied with a qualifier like 'created by' followed by the manufacturer's name. Because you can't say the word diamond on its own – that can make it harder to rank for that keyword.

Of course, the FTC wants to make sure that people don't advertise non-mined diamonds as mined diamonds. Yet, man-made diamonds have the same chemical properties as mined diamonds, the main difference is the point of origin, as they are created in a laboratory. And that's most interesting because we know many people have been killed working in diamond mines and there's a lot of local conflict over these resources. That's why it's important to educate customers on the brand's values in every piece of content.

There are also keywords that we can't use even though other lab-grown diamond brands use them, as those terms are not on-brand for us. We have specific brand guidelines to follow when creating content or promoting the products to make our brand stand apart, which can be challenging when leading the SEO strategy. Another one of our brand values is that all our products are 'gender-neutral', which is another great thing to stand for. But it's not a keyword to optimise for from an SEO perspective, because most people are still searching for 'women's jewellery' and 'men's jewellery'.

So, when you start keyword research, you often already have an idea of what keyword to type, and then you get suggestions based on that. But for this, you have to think, 'if they're looking for gender-neutral jewellery, what are they searching for? What are the terms they're using?'. So we use the word 'unisex', but there aren't a lot of searches for that, either. It's quite challenging being ahead of the market, in this way. And so this means you still have to find ways to incorporate the high-volume search terms, so that you still bring traffic.

## Educating the business

Another big challenge, especially if you work for high-end retail or ecommerce sites, is they tend to prioritise imagery and photography on their website, versus text, to try to ensure a clean design. But when you do SEO, you may have to add copy to the site so that you can rank for your targeted keywords.

So, for instance, you may suggest adding links to the navigation, but your stakeholders say, 'no, the navigation doesn't look good if it has too many links', even if it makes sense for users and from an SEO perspective. Or they might remove copy from the header, because too much copy doesn't look good. So you always have to find the right balance between the copy and design needs.

At VRAI, the solution that I found was creating new category-page templates where we can incorporate more copy and add images to keep the page visually appealing, shoppable and SEO-friendly at the same time. So we now have FAQs on product-listing pages, where you have to click to expand the tabs for more information, but it doesn't look like there's too much copy on the page. It looks good, but you've still incorporated the content you need.

One of the other big challenges is letting other teams know that they need to think about SEO for anything that could impact the website's rankings and traffic. You have to constantly communicate with other departments and make sure you're involved in any meeting about any website updates that could affect the rankings. So there's a lot of education internally too.

And the way you communicate with every team is different, because they have different needs. For instance, when I talk to the ecommerce team, I would say 'okay, when you upload new products on the site, you have to make sure you use this exact product name, that the meta title is optimised and the URL has this structure'. This is what they care about when it comes to their job.

And the design team – they should really get you to review any new page design they create to ensure there is no impact on Google's ability to crawl and index the site. Any project like this should be SEO-driven and it's important to communicate your expectations. For instance, you can create briefs where you provide the SEO guidelines and search data to the designers before they begin. SEO is all about providing the best search experience, and that's not only about having people land on your website, but also having them convert. Sometimes people might think, 'SEO and UX are not the same', but they have a lot more overlap than most people think.

Most stakeholders don't know the data that you have as an SEO, so someone may say, 'why don't we build a page about this, because our competitors have one?'. But then you may have to explain, 'I don't recommend doing that. Because there are no searches for that keyword. If your goal is to increase traffic, then I wouldn't create that page, I would build another page, on that other topic'.

This can be about going right back to basics, educating the business about how search engines work, what we can control and especially what we can't control on Google. For instance, when I got a request from the CEO to feature more thumbnail images in our search results, I had to explain that, whether it's thumbnails, meta descriptions or featured snippets, there is no guarantee Google will display them, even when we optimise the site for this.

That's also an opportunity to conduct your own research as you can't expect to find Google documentation that will tell you what to do to guarantee a certain search feature. So one way to improve your search presence is through comparing search results, looking for common patterns between sites and testing different features.

These are challenges that I think any in-house SEO has, but I like that SEO is a constant learning process. In this role, it's a real opportunity to influence and educate other teams, so that everyone is on board with the kind of strategy we need for a brand like VRAI. And when you see positive results, you build trust and can drive even more changes that will impact the business.

# OKRs – where business, team and SEO strategy meet

## STEFAN MUSTIELES

### SENIOR ORGANIC SEO MANAGER, PRIORY GROUP

With more than a decade of SEO experience, Stefan has worked in-house at brands such as MoneySupermarket.com, Shop Direct and, currently, at Priory. During his time on the agency side, he also worked closely with brands such as Tesco and Regatta as an extension of their in-house SEO teams. Stefan has worked in a number of different industries, but his favourite has always been ecommerce. He specialises in SEO strategy and believes the key to being successful at any in-house role is to align your SEO goals with those of the business. Stefan does this by implementing OKRs (Objectives and Key Results).

I started my SEO career at MoneySuperMarket.com. I set up the gas and electricity customer-service team at the call centre. They were a powerhouse in organic SEO at the time, and they wanted to increase the size of the team, and realised the best way to do that was to hire from within. So they set up what was called a Search Academy. And that brought people from within the business, from all different areas of the business, to learn SEO. And that's where I learned my trade.

Coming from customer service, we understood what the needs of the customer were, what the pain points were in the online journey. When I started doing SEO, I was working on the energy and home-insurance parts of the site and it was great to be able to call on that experience to improve things. A background in speaking with customers over the phone was also helpful when tackling the link-building aspect, because we were able to communicate with bloggers and site owners, in terms of getting relevant link acquisition as well.

I went from MoneySuperMarket to Shop Direct, where I kind of jumped in at the deep end with such a huge ecommerce site. They've got Littlewoods.com and Very.co.uk, hundreds of thousands of URLs, ecommerce facets and filters. It was a great place to really learn about and specialise in technical SEO. That's also where I kind of fell in love with working in ecommerce, but I wanted to carry on learning different niches. So that's where my career has taken me, to lots of different types of websites, whether that's lead generation, SME, affiliate marketing. What's kept me in SEO is learning about these different areas and understanding what's important to those businesses.

One of my biggest past successes was working on Broadway Basketeers, a small, niche site that specialised in Kosher gift baskets. Trying to get cut through for them against the large brands in the gift-basket market, such as Harry & David, or GourmetGiftBaskets.com, 1800Baskets, was very difficult. But, through changing the strategy, we were able to rank for 'Christmas basket' terms at the right time of year, when customers started shopping. We were in really high positions and kind of disrupted the top-five competitors, they really didn't see us coming.

We did this through a strategy where, the previous Christmas, we saw a change in how Google was ranking sites. For the head terms, such as 'Christmas baskets', or 'Christmas gift baskets', Google understood that the intent for the customers was more around researching things like the different brands and which types of baskets they wanted. We were never going to rank our Product Listings Page (PLP) against the bigger players in the market, so we changed the strategy to create more informational content, like the 'best 10 Christmas gift baskets for you to enjoy'. It was more of a listicle-type article and that directly matched what Google believed the intent was for that SERP, which allowed us to rank. So it was about being able to see what's going on with the SERP, and then react accordingly and set strategy.

At Priory Group – a large percentage of their traffic relies on organic search – mainly through informational content, in terms of self-help, getting help with depression, signs and symptoms of certain mental illnesses or addictions. Then there's the more transactional content, where we try to get the customers the help they need.

I've been here now since July 2021 and we have implemented an SEO strategy where we are growing the transactional content. It is a longer customer journey, and previous strategies focused a lot on the informational content and driving a lot of traffic. So we've now pivoted to focus more on that transactional content, to try to get more inquiries through the door. Sometimes we get leads in, whether it's through a form fill or a phone call, and, half of the time, those potential customers don't realise the cost involved. So there's an educational part of it as well, where we have to make sure our content spells out that, either they have to be referred to Priory, or they can get help through payment plans and things like that. I am pleased to say that Priory is currently seeing its highest ever organic visibility, so the strategy is working.

In terms of other projects in-house here, the biggest one we've got coming up is a huge migration from our current CMS, and also some migrations of the smaller websites that we own, to merge them with the bigger website that we have at Priory. I'm leading on this, with our development agency, because there's a lot of SEO implications, and we're aiming to deliver in 2023.

The biggest challenge, whenever I've been in-house, is capacity – and being able to get those resources signed off. It's often lots of different teams fighting for capacity, especially development, whether that's the commercial team trying to get a specific banner on the top of their product pages, or the PPC team trying to get certain tracking codes implemented. I love doing technical audits and seeing the changes implemented by the development team, but also creating relationships with those different teams. That's a key part of technical SEO, to try to get your changes through, and have that conversation with them about what their capabilities and what their limitations are.

Overall, SEO strategy is what I'm known for and it's something I learned early on in my career. With in-house SEO, there's often lots of different teams you're working with, all with their own objectives. In the past, in different places I've worked, SEOs had their own objectives too – and it might be to grow traffic by 10%, or grow organic lead volume by 15%. But, when you're trying to work with other teams, maybe the development team or the commercial team, that SEO metric doesn't mean anything to them. Ultimately, this work should be governed by a business objective, but sometimes even that business objective can also be quite 'wishy washy', there's no true metrics assigned to it.

OBJECTIVE AND KEY RESULTS

That's why I really like the Objectives and Key Results (OKRs) methodology, where you have your SEO metrics tied into an overall business objective, which means something to other teams, and helps when you're trying to get buy-in for certain tasks. At Priory, one of our business objectives is to grow our market share within the addictions and mental-health niche. Below is an example of one of our OKRs.

| Objective A | Grow our market share in key mental health & addictions battlegrounds |
| --- | --- |
| Key Result 1 | Increase Organic Traffic YoY by 10% |
| Key Result 2 | Climb into top 10 for addictions market share |
| Key Result 3 | Climb into top 15 for mental health market share |
| Key Result 4 | Increase overall SEO visibility past its previous best |

So it's about how you break that objective down into what's going to matter to us, from an SEO point of view. Using OKRs, you can have that overarching business objective, then your key results are what you measure as an SEO and build into your monthly reporting. We can expand upon this further to include 'Key Actions'. These are the actual tasks that you are going to do on a monthly basis to achieve each key result.

| Objective A | Grow our market share in key mental health & addictions battlegrounds |
| --- | --- |
| Key Result 1 | Increase Organic Traffic YoY by 10% |
| Key Action 1 | Restructure content on core category pages |
| Key Action 2 | Highlight large volume, low competition KWs in 11-20 |
| Key Action 3 | Competitor gap analysis to highlight missing content topics |
| Key Result 2 | Climb into top 10 for addictions market share |
| Key Result 3 | Climb into top 15 for mental health market share |
| Key Result 4 | Increase overall SEO visibility past its previous best |

So now, our SEO strategy is clear. We know what we need to do to hit each key result, and by achieving all key results, this should help us achieve our overall business objective. At end of year reviews, this will go a long way into showing what you have achieved as an individual or as a team and how SEO has been instrumental in helping the business achieve its overall objectives.

SEO sometimes lives in its own little bubble, especially on Twitter. And I think we need to do better at 'PRing' SEO, within a business. A lot of people in big-brand organisations, and it was the same at Shop Direct, it's the same here at Priory, they just take SEO as a given, especially when it comes down to brand search. And what I'd like to see change in the future is for SEOs, especially in-house, is people taking the time to PR SEO – doing more presentations to the wider business on the importance of SEO, but also showing how other teams can help with SEO. One very common area is the PR team, who are often just interested in press releases, which is of course about getting visibility for the brand. So it's about making sure that they know they can help you, in terms of inserting links into the press releases or including certain keywords, for example. Or how SEO can help the commercial teams reach their goals by giving them insight through keyword research of the most popular product searches. And that's where it comes back to the OKRs. Where your metrics and your key results and objectives are all tied into that business objective, it can actually help you get more of that capacity.

# Why topical authority is not what you think it is (and why it's going to change again soon)

## MORDY OBERSTEIN
### HEAD OF SEO BRANDING, WIX.COM

---

Israel-based SEO veteran Mordy has used his expertise to help develop some of the industry's most important tools, from website-builder WIX, to Semrush, and back again. He's currently creating a course to help WIX users master their own SEO, but is also in the weeds supporting small businesses to build their search profiles.

---

Recently, I've been dealing with a case where a product lost a lot of rankings – at the hands of one of the algorithm updates. And I've been trying to figure out like, 'why? The content is good'. There was a strong cluster of content around the product. There were blog posts about it, documentation about it, landing pages, so why did the site lose ranking? And one of the reasons why I think it did, and this could really apply to any site, is a misconception about what it means to be an 'authority' on a topic today.

I think SEOs in general, and certainly SEOs in the past, would say 'okay, I'll write around a content cluster, I'll write a lot about this particular topic. Google will think our website has a huge section about this topic – we must be an authority about it – and I have my internal linking setup and it all goes back to this main cluster page. That's all very good'. And that is all really good, for Google understanding the content and the structure of your page, and how much content you have and the content you have around that particular topic. I definitely agree that's a good thing to do.

But if being a topical authority is your goal, I don't think it simply works like that anymore, because of the way that Google uses machine learning. What machine learning basically does, and what Google and their search advocate John Mueller have seemingly been alluding to is, 'we look at different verticals. And we look at how content is talked about in different verticals. And content in one vertical may look and feel and sound very different to content in a different vertical. We want to make sure that your site talks about the topic in a way that it's meant to be talked about'. And this is just the way machine learning works – it takes a dataset, it inputs the information, it says, 'okay, for this, this is how we think content should look, or how the page should look and feel'.

Obviously everything depends on your vertical, but whatever that is, you now have to really align to how Google sees content for that topic. Health and finance are obvious examples. Google looks at that very differently. The health vertical is really the epitome of sites that get killed by updates. If they're a health information site but use informational content as a way to segue you into buying their products, Google's looking at this and profiling it and thinking, 'maybe this doesn't line up here?'. And once Google has that question on a topic around health information, it's going to be like 'this content may be great but we're not ranking it'. And you can literally see this happen to certain websites.

At the same time, when Google releases an update, they may just say, 'look, sometimes you're just not relevant for queries anymore. The user intent changed'. The classic example would be if you have a whole site about media that talks about VHS, but no one's interested in VHS anymore. But it doesn't have to be that extreme. It could be the user profile around certain types of commercial queries, like Google's noticed that users want a little bit more additional, informational content around the product you're selling. So the profile's changed.

That's why I think profiling where you lost keywords is really important. Are there similar keywords that you lost? Did you gain other keywords? What kind of pages are now ranking that didn't rank before? What's different about them? To me, it takes a lot of profiling on your side too, which is, in fact, a lot of guesswork. I think, as SEOs, we've always thought 'here's the answer, here's the one reason why Google is doing this'. But I can look at something that has happened and be like, 'here's 10 reasons why I think the content that's ranking now is different'.

Glenn Gabe, a huge SEO expert in the United States, says 'throw the kitchen sink at it'. And I totally agree. You see a problem? Go for it. But don't stop there. What other problems do you see? Because you don't know what might be the deciding factor with Google. The general point for topical authority is that Google's not just looking at how much content you have, or how well-established your brand is, or how many content clusters you have around a topic. They're really profiling things, because machine learning works by profiling. It's taking an input, and it's matching up, to say 'okay, this is what we want, does your profile match our profile?'. And if our pages are just basically landing pages, even though they're linking to deeper pages, if they're purely trying to be acquisition pages without offering an FAQ or something more, Google is like 'no, you're not going to rank as highly as other pages that do this'. It's happened to us in a bunch of verticals, and if you look at what's out there on the SERP, you can see the intent has changed and Google has essentially said, 'this is different now, your profile doesn't match up the same way'.

## The future of topical authority

So let's take the Google MUM update, it's still being developed, but it's going to be injected in the algorithm way more often, I would assume. And it presents a different way of understanding content. It's a different way of understanding what's good for a user. The example they give is 'I hiked Mount Adams, I want to hike Mount Fuji in the fall, what do I need to prepare differently?'.

And now, Google parses all of this, they parse 'comparing Adams to Fuji', they parse 'unique characteristics of hiking and Autumn' and the word 'differently'. And then they parse what it means 'to prepare?'. Does that mean the equipment that you need? Or does that mean training? And MUM will be able to identify, it means both training and equipment, and it will show both access points to results about equipment and access points to results about training. Like, that's crazy. That's awesome. That's really smart. But that means to Google, if you have the website 'prepareforhiking.com', and you only talk about equipment, you're automatically showing you're missing part of the content profile. So there's nothing wrong with your page. It just doesn't align to how Google understands intent anymore. And Google is always changing how well it can do these kinds of things. So if you want to be a topical authority, you have to constantly align your site to how Google understands and profiles that topic.

I would like to see Google talk more about this kind of stuff. And I'm not putting them down – John Mueller does a great job. And there's only so much I think that John can or can't say or does or doesn't know. It's machine learning and they've said themselves 'we don't know the algorithm, it's run through a ton of machine learning properties. And it's constantly recalibrating. We can't say that "this is the algorithm"'.

But you know, they'll talk about writing 'good content' and I would like to hear them talk more about what does good content mean to you? How do you decide on what is good content? One of the topics that often comes up among SEOs is, they have the Quality Rater guidelines, people who are actually looking at sites, rating them for quality, and sending Google back information that Google tries to use algorithmically, potentially. And there's a lot of talk about, well, 'how do they impact the algorithm?'. I would love to hear Google talk more about 'here's a case where we had a bunch of information from Quality Rater guidelines. And here's how we do this algorithmically. Here's how we simulate that, because we can't do it as a person, because we can't qualitatively understand information'. And they've talked about how they have signals that try to imitate how somebody will look at quality. But, give us a hardcore, a concrete example – 'here's what that actually looks like'.

Because there's definitely a content gap. Google might return 4 million results in 2.3 seconds. But a lot of that's crap. I understand why they don't want to tell me about how the link algorithm works. But, if you're just telling me what you think is good content then I'll write good content. Tell me what you want, so I can give it to you.

# Are you making a good first – and lasting – impression with your app-store optimisation?

## REJOICE OJIAKU
### CO-FOUNDER, B-DIGITALUK

Rejoice started her career on a graduate scheme with Beamly, where they rotated staff every six months, but she started with, loved and stuck with SEO. She's had experience in all aspects of SEO – but loves putting herself in the consumer's shoes when it comes to creating content. In 2020, Rejoice co-founded B-DigitalUK, which aims to get more Black people into the creative industries, and is interested in how understanding the digital world is when it comes to people from other cultures. She's keen for more companies to create more programmes to get people in at the entry-level and hopes to turn B-Digital into a digital agency.

I think a lot more companies should consider their App Store Optimisation (ASO). So if you are a brand that has a website, but you also have an app people can download, you want to make sure you're doing everything you can to ensure that's being found. Especially if you speak about your app on your website, you need to make sure they're working quite well together.

Not every client I work with will request to do app-store optimisation. And I guess it depends on how well you feel you're performing, in terms of the ASO world. A lot of clients tend to focus mostly on search ads, so they do quite a lot of paid campaigns for the apps. They'll think about how, organically, their website is being found, but not how, organically, their app is found.

## The basics

ASO is essentially the process of optimising your mobile apps to rank higher within app-store search. And it fits nicely into SEO because there's still the concept of metadata. But in ASO, you're looking at things like the app name, the app title and app description, all of that feeds into any ranking factor.

And, when we're doing SEO, a lot of people focus on Google or Bing. With ASO, we're still looking at Google and its Play store, but we enter the realm of Apple search – and so you've now entered two ecosystems.

It's still all about search functionalities. And so it's interesting how we can take what we learn from SEO into ASO search. There's different guidelines, but Google Play kind of mimics how Google works on desktop.

For Apple, keywords are still important. But the difference is how we optimise keywords for our title and description. For Apple, it gives you a keyword field where you place those keywords, and we can even utilise competitors' names as keywords. It's really a trick, so whenever people search for your competitors, they are going to bring your app up too.

Another difference with an Apple search is, even though it has the field called 'app description', Apple doesn't consider that as a ranking factor. So you can write whatever you want, it's not going to help you rank. On Google Play, it has a long description, short description and those are ranking factors. And you would want to put your keywords within those descriptors for Google Play. For Apple, there isn't really a concept of 'targeted keywords', the same way we see it as Google Play. If you have a targeted keyword here, naturally, you want to put that into the title, put that into the description. For Apple, they're just putting the keyword field and 'we'll do the rest'.

With Apple, everything else has to be more of a creative approach. Obviously, you need to have your name, and any promotional text to be catchy. But I think Apple does focus a lot on the design, your screenshots, your videos, how is that looking?

I work closely with the paid search team to look at intent around the app stores. So, what we tend to do is, discuss what keywords they have found people are using and that have quite good conversions. Then I will look at it from an organic perspective, in terms of how well I can fit that within the metadata. Because, we know 'this' keyword would have given us 'this' amount of downloads, so then I try to find a way to look at it from a data perspective and embed it into something like a long description or promotional texts.

And we'll test it out. So we change the metadata, maybe give it a month and see if that increases downloads, if it has an effect on the category rankings, if it has an effect on where they rank for certain keywords. And then we can decide 'should we keep this, should we not?'.

# Backlinks

We worked with one brand doing backlink analysis for apps – again, something brands may think of for SEO – but perhaps something that they don't know can be important when it comes to apps. But it is important, especially from the Google side of things. If Google allows backlinks for your website, they will take into account backlinks that lead to your download page.

We saw that the brand had quite bad Citation and Trust Flow compared to competitors, using this metric on the Majestic SEO tool. Trust Flow analyses how trustworthy your site is by measuring its quality. So, according to Majestic at the time, the brand's app had a Trust Flow that was 15 – and the closer you get to 100 – the better. And the Citation Flow mostly looks at the popularity of the destination. And so, if you have a very high Citation Flow, for example, on your homepage link, it means that your home page URL is popular, especially if more reputable sites keep linking back to it. And Google is going to say 'okay, well, all these really good pages are linking back to it. This must be a good site'.

So we started testing a digital PR strategy for their apps – to drive links back to the download page, in order to see if we get more instals, and if that's going to have an impact on the backlink profile. We decided we wouldn't work with any publishing brands with a Domain Authority below 40, but we were testing it out with different publications for three months. And we were lucky, because we were getting brands linking to us that were between the 60s and 90s.

And after the three months, we saw that the brand went from a Trust Flow of 15 up to 40. So we were able to make the app look more trustworthy and people looking for it could download it and know it is trusted.

They had a really good backlink analysis and each month we were getting at least 10 new instals, organically. And this was something we were just testing out, we didn't know if it would work. We just said 'let's see if we can do this and improve it'.

The brand was particularly happy with the backlink analysis. They just wanted to clean up the backlink profile – and they saw quite reputable sites were linking back to them – in the US market.

With the backlinks, this is about generating awareness of your app, or the awareness of whatever category your app falls in. It would be pointless if you have all these great backlinks and then when people actually go to download your app, it's completely useless, it doesn't work, it's not optimised. So you kind of have to balance them both.

You have to ensure that your app is actually optimised well, you do have the right creatives, but also make sure the ratings are awesome. You can't have a very good backlink profile and your app rating is two. That contradicts itself from a user perspective anyway, so one doesn't directly affect the other, but it's just good to make sure that there's a balance between optimisation and quality, if you're trying to drive people to download the app.

## Some pitfalls

So there are mistakes that I see a lot of brands make, in terms of creative. One is around consistency. It's like they don't necessarily think about how a user is going to meet you at your first impression. So for instance, you have an app on Google Play and then you have an app on Apple Store, where if you look at the creative, the screenshots, it looks like two different brands and there's no synergy. That's not to say there will be really negative effects on your ranking. But you have to show you're thinking about your consumers. You want to show the same features to everyone. You don't want to isolate one set of consumers and do all your great creatives on the Apple Store and forget Google Play.

Another thing that I tend to see is that brands think they know better than the creatives that work for them – who happen to be specialists in design, brand imagery and formats. So, once you've handed over your requirements – take a step back – let the creatives actually work with what you've given them. There's no point hovering around them. Otherwise you should do it and not have a creative team. I see a lot of creatives get frustrated at that, they just want to get on with it and show you the first draft. Then we can start making the amendments. Rather than tweaking throughout the process, because that means you're going to slow it down and delay any launch dates that you have.

Brands also need to think more about the concept of A/B testing, when it comes to your creatives, your videos and screenshots, your app icon. Brands do not A/B test enough, so you don't actually know what is working for you. It's more encouraged when working with a search team, but I know creatives would always welcome A/B tests too. But – importantly – don't test five things at once. Let's try, maybe, one call-to-action. Does it work? If not, remove it and try something else.

More generally for me – the biggest challenge I've experienced when it comes to working with clients – is when you are working on ASO, SEO, any project, and there's this non-clarity about who the stakeholders are. Then, when you start going in to ask for approval, there is this 'red tape' – you ask the person who you thought was in charge and they have to get approval from two other people. Which again delays the project.

So it's always good in the beginning to make sure to find out from the clients – 'who are the full stakeholders involved?'. So I know who I need to copy into emails, who to send reports to. This means we can all get things done much quicker.

# It's time to talk about how much we get paid – and it's not about how much you know about SEO

## DOMINIK SCHWARZ
### CHIEF INBOUND OFFICER, HOMETOGO

Dominik started building websites when he was 13. His long history of working in the online industry spans corporate and agency roles, working on SEO alongside marketing and strategy. He now heads up inbound marketing as Chief Inbound Officer at holiday-rentals leader HomeToGo, alongside leading Vertical Inhouse, an organisation that provides resources for in-house SEOs. As a longstanding champion of in-house SEO, he's rounding off his three-part contribution to this book series on why and how SEOs need to professionalise.

I have been in SEO for 17 years now, since 2005 and I'm so happy still, after many years in this industry, because I think things are only getting dramatically, drastically better. Google claimed for 20 years that it's quality that makes you rank really well. And for a long time in history, that was simply a lie. Of course, that was what they intended to do, but they weren't capable of doing it.

Now in the last couple of years, finally, for the very first time, the often dirty tricks don't work anymore. And that's great, because we're all users of Google, and what that now means is the website that works most sustainably, on quality, is ranking best and making the web a little bit better.

Good SEO is the combination of good information architecture, and on top, good user interactions, and on top, recommendations from third parties, or backlinks, and on top, of course, the content that lives on the site. And for me, all of these different parts are things you do not achieve with 'budget', but with investment. You invest in faster websites, in user research, in better design.

SEO is not simply a 'marketing channel', where you put budget in and traffic comes in, then you turn it off and the traffic is gone. A marketing channel is something where you put budget and you can clearly measure 'how much revenue does the work of this channel result in'.

In SEO, it's different, it has a compounding effect. You have so many different areas and fields of work that, way too often, you can't really quantify – making the website a little bit more beautiful – how much more money does it make you? How much more money does it make you to have a better information architecture? You can, as a sum of all of it together, quantify, of course, that 'my SEO in 2022 is so much better than in 2021'. But it is a whole ecosystem that works together.

That means, today, SEO also represents a broad set of skills. It's about technology. It's about understanding users. It's about understanding design. It's about information architecture. It's about so many different things. And, because of this, the people who work in SEO are not equal to 'marketing budget', either. Of course, SEO is not free, in the sense it doesn't cost anything on the bottom line. But it's a completely different kind of money you spend, from a financial perspective, from other areas of marketing.

If I am able, as an SEO person can, to generate a potential share of traffic that leads to a substantial percentage of revenue, then we also need to understand that the traffic that is coming through SEO, or the revenue that is coming through SEO, is in most cases, the margin a company can work with. Even if the traffic that comes through SEO is a minor share, say it's 20% of all the company's traffic, that 20% of SEO revenue is often the margin the company has to play with. Meanwhile, the performance marketing part, in most growth companies, more or less equals zero. You spend as much as you can, and whatever comes in is going out immediately into more ad spend.

## The data-driven case for better pay

I often speak about how SEO people need to professionalise – we need to talk on an eye level with the other people at the table, on the board. If we agree that SEO, first of all, is a set of skills that is extremely broad. And second, that it's extremely crucial in companies, integrated throughout basically all processes, SEOs can and should demand a seat at the table. And we should be paid adequately, and equally, to other professionals and professions that oversee such large parts of a company.

I have just run, for the second time since 2018, a representative study to gather German salary data in SEO, and this can help us all understand who is better paid, or worse paid, when it comes to SEO. And why. This gives us a couple of rules of thumbs that can help when negotiating SEO salary.

First of all, experience pays, as in all jobs, of course. But in SEO, the salary levels go up quite dramatically after the first five years of experience. We cluster experience between zero to five years, five years to 10 years, then

10 years or more. And we see a huge step up after your entry-level job. So the longer you are in the industry, of course, the better.

The second thing we see is, the bigger the company, the better the salaries are. So organisations that have more than 1,500 people have way higher median salaries than smaller companies. However, there may be outliers. We see a way bigger salary spread in super-small companies, where five to 10 people work on a product and do that extremely successfully. Here, you might not earn as much as at the big corporates, but you could gain greater influence here so that your share of the work is seen. So you can negotiate really well, in these startups. When we look across industries, we see the typical patterns – so within media, the salaries are the lowest. Marketing, media, design, PR, publishing houses are at the lower end. While automobile, banks and so on, are industries that typically pay better.

What does not correlate too much with SEO salary is your education. Interestingly, having some mid-level education pays best, way better than a Masters, Bachelor or even PhD. But the single biggest differences in salaries are a) if you have your own team, and b) if you are end-to-end responsible for that team. So not only giving topical guidance, but if you decide on your team's salaries, manage performance and you own the P&L for your team. Here, we see the biggest difference in salaries, 25% and more, once you are in a situation where you have end-to-end team ownership. And the larger your team, the better your salary. That's not very surprising. But we've seen that in the data super clearly.

It's hard to pin down 'the' SEO salary, because it depends on all these different factors. But overall, the takeaway is that the median person in SEO is earning 'so so'. So, if you're not leading a team, then you are mid-level paid. I believe we are all underpaid, though, because it is a job that is more challenging, more broad and needs much more education than if you specialise in a certain kind of paid marketing channel, or email marketing.

Really then, the path to a good salary in SEO is building up your team, leading it and owning responsibility. And this makes it quite clear that, ultimately, it's not the 'best SEO' who earns the most, but the best process manager, the best negotiator, the best manager. And this fits neatly with the argument that professionalising SEO careers means stepping up – not doing every single optimisation yourself anymore – but selling your team's work, implementing processes and negotiating with other teams to support certain tasks. That's the bigger driver for success, and therefore salary, than being the best in SEO trivia.

That means learning to speak the same language as other people on the board is crucial. You can't join a board meeting and tell people something about 'visibility', that's not the currency they think in. You need to understand that people are interested in 'market share', 'how much of the whole market do we get with our SEO?'. That's a question people ask, because they need to have something that they can compare it to. You need to prove that it's worth having an SEO on the board. You need to prove that there is bottom-line revenue coming in through your channel. And understanding this means you can push things through, and against people. But you also need to make people excited about it, to enable them to fight for you. That is extremely important. And you can achieve that through education.

## Data-driven salaries?

I get hundreds of requests from people asking me to send over the survey data. And I get a lot of feedback from big companies that say, 'we use the data as baseline data in all of our talks for salaries', which is great, because that makes the work worth doing.

As a manager, you need to know the market value of your people to make them stay at your company. There's nothing more important than that. And of course, yoga courses are not enough when the salary is just too low compared to other jobs. It's an extremely important factor to be paid fairly. So it's important for managers. But it is also important for everyone working in the industry to have a benchmark – you need to be able to pinpoint a certain dot in the study and say, 'well, people with my experience in this field are earning that much on average, why am I 20% below?'. And I get a lot of feedback from people who say they used the data to renegotiate their salary.

There should be an inflow of people coming into our industry and there isn't. And I see two things. First of all, SEO has a bad reputation, and it's our own fault, because the whole industry tried to make a secret out of SEO for too many years. So people who are serious about honest work might not think about SEO in the first place. That's our problem to fix. And one part of that is paying a fair amount for important work.

Secondly, I believe there's no other set of skills in digital marketing where you learn so many completely different things. I feel very fortunate that, after this many years, I still learn something every day. For me, it's a job where there's always some different problem and I get to tackle it. That's an opportunity we should shout about.

Somebody who understands SEO understands a lot of areas of a business, and so if you don't want to stay, you can progress into being a product manager, a marketing manager, a CEO. All of these career paths are completely logical steps. Because it's also true that every SEO person is, to a certain extent, a CPO, a CEO, taking on aspects of all of these overarching positions at once.

It's time we take our seats at the board and pay our teams what they're worth.

# The headlines from a decade doing SEO in the publishing industry

## CARLY STEVEN

### HEAD OF SEO, THE SUN

An experienced SEO in British publishing, Carly joined the
Daily Mail in 2007. After this, she left the UK to work in Canada,
starting as an SEO consultant at the Montreal Gazette. Carly
came back to an Audience Development role at CityAM in 2014,
before joining News UK two years later. She is co-chair of the
Association of Online Publishers' Audience Development group.

SEO has definitely had an impact on the news industry. I don't think anywhere I've worked, editorial has been led by SEO, but it should always be SEO informed. If we can see through SEO that people are particularly interested in one aspect of a story, then we might write another story about that, because we know that people are searching for that information.

Most newsrooms now produce explainers, based on the questions people are asking Google. A few years ago, hardly anybody was doing that. I hate when people say 'it's for Google'. I don't think that's true, it's for the humans using Google, using insights that we get through SEO.

It's such a basic human thing – if you can show editors and reporters that more people are reading their stories, they're naturally more inclined to listen, adopt best practices and think about the headlines for search, as well as social and the other referrers they care about.

To me, it has influenced newsrooms to work really well together. We have a really healthy relationship between the audience department and editorial, a two-way conversation – 'is this right for our audience? Will it drive traffic? Is it a good story?' are fundamentally the most important questions.

## At the heart of the newsroom

The audience department is right at the heart of The Sun's newsroom today. We're involved in all the news conferences. I like to think we're very respected within the newsroom, as a department. All in all, our audience team is about 20 people. We have a team of audience managers and data analysts. We also have a head of SEO and a head of social, and then teams that sit underneath us. Then we have the US operation, which is separate, and includes an audience team of social and SEO.

At The Sun, when I first started, it was basically just me, and we've built up the team from there. Obviously people have come and gone, but we've been able to see something grow from nothing – because before that, we were behind a paywall, so there wasn't a need for an SEO department.

In some respects, SEO is getting harder and harder and harder to do. I look back at when I first started – it didn't feel easy at the time – but relative to now, it was a lot more straightforward. When Core Web Vitals rolled out last summer, Google's big change in page experience, that was a huge challenge for the industry.

And because of that, we've made some really big improvements as a site. Even something like the motoring section, we've looked at the potential, come up with a strategy, then implemented it. That has resulted in significant increases in search traffic, which has been very satisfying. But one of the most rewarding things to come out of that is that different parts of the business have come together and started to collaborate.

Today, we work so closely with the performance team, with technical teams, with commercial teams, having to be really sophisticated in planning our strategies. I couldn't have imagined the conversations that we have now, a couple of years ago.

With Core Web Vitals becoming a ranking factor, there's nothing we can do as SEOs to control the performance of our pages. So we have to work more collaboratively with other departments, and other publishers, as well. It's our performance team that is looking at the performance of the site, the Core Web Vitals, metrics, page-experience metrics, basically making sure the site is as fast and as user-friendly as possible.

We've got very specific metrics, targets and thresholds that we need to meet in order to get as many of our pages into as good a category as we can. Then we can compare ourselves to other publishers for each of those metrics. I'm sure most publishers are waiting every month for that. But for me, what we have is a very strong, very well-integrated, highly productive and efficient team. And, for me, personally, that's the thing I'm most proud of.

The Core Web Vitals change has also brought conversations about ads right to the fore, because so much of the essence behind it is about page experience. Ads can make the difference between a good experience and a bad experience.

One of the Core Web Vitals metrics that we care about a lot is Cumulative Layout Shift (CLS), which is stuff moving on the page because things are loading, that could be ads, videos, images. So absolutely, we care about it. You obviously need both – we can't have a free website without ads – but getting that balance right, between the ads that generate the revenue and the page experience for a reader, is hugely important.

And we've made loads of improvements and really positive strides, like when you have a featured video at the top of a story, what impact does that have for page experience? What can we do technically with the infrastructure behind that to improve page-load times, to have a positive impact on those Core Web Vitals metrics?

Because they're a ranking factor, we care a lot about them, from an SEO point of view. They can make the difference between us ranking for a story, or somebody else. It's something we're having really frank conversations about all the time. Similarly, we're now getting to the point where, if the image that appears in that top story is better than somebody else's, people are more likely to click on it. It's that sort of thing that now makes a difference.

The other thing that is really important from an image point of view is Google Discover, which is, again, a bit of a game-changer for a lot of publishers. There isn't much explicit guidance about optimising for Discover, but one thing we do know is that high-quality images are hugely important, so this is something we've really tried to focus on.

## Top stories?

There was also quite a significant change in the layout of 'top stories' on mobile in early 2021 that had a pretty significant impact on us – and I think a lot of publishers. It's basically gone from four slots where you could rank, to only one.

Google is also prioritising local news a lot more, so there are more publishers battling for that one spot, it's all become a lot harder. That means a lot of publishers are now thinking that we shouldn't put all our emphasis on top stories, which is the very obvious place for news publishers to want to rank, so we are also caring more about the evergreen.

It's about getting that regular trickle of traffic that comes from good organic rankings, a nice kind of cushion against any kind of volatility that we've seen. Having a strategy around both is just sensible. Once you can identify the topics you care about, that's where there is that opportunity. It's something we're putting increasing amounts of effort into.

We've done a lot of experimenting around liveblogs, which can have high SEO value, as well as driving engagement and keeping people on the site. Having said that, you do need to think carefully about the topics that lend themselves to live blogs – sometimes there's just not enough content to make them useful to our readers – which is obviously critical, even if they might rank well.

Most publishers will have structured data that tells Google 'this is a liveblog', because for certain types of live events, Google recognises them as the best way of informing readers. The Guardian has done some really great work around that, there's some really interesting things around pinning things to the top of liveblogs and the technology behind that. I think a lot of publishers that maybe haven't previously invested much in liveblogs are seeing the opportunities.

It's just about getting that balance, right between, 'yes, there's lots of search, let's do a liveblog' and 'well actually like, is this the best way of telling that story?'. Making sure you can answer 'yes' to both of those questions.

## Audience?

SEO is naturally about reaching new people when they're searching for information about a certain topic – so engaging and retaining repeat users is a real challenge. We know that SEO is very good at hitting people once and not necessarily keeping them, it's not the obvious referer for loyal and engaged users. But, we try not to just see SEO as a way of reaching new people, but also, then converting them to become those really valuable people, because they're going to come back to the site again.

We work very closely with the analytics team in defining those metrics and trying to work out new ways of engaging people that come in through those channels like SEO – coming up with new innovative ways of recirculating them back through the website.

Ultimately, that's about getting direct traffic, getting people caring so much about the brand that they come to us first.

## What's on the agenda at the Association of Online Publishers?

The Audience Development steering group is basically a bunch of people from a diverse group of publishers, coming together every month to talk about things that are impacting our industry.

It's a really helpful, constructive platform for having conversations like, 'what does your audience team look like?'. Because of some of the challenges we have faced with algorithm changes, Core Web Vitals, external factors beyond our control, it's actually brought publishers together a lot more. Certainly from an audience perspective.

Traffic is always on the agenda. And I think we will always want to compare notes on things that are difficult to optimise for. Google Discover is something we always want to talk about, because it can be really volatile. Algorithm updates, inevitably, like 'what did you see?'.

One of the other challenges that the industry is grappling with at the moment is AMP – we're all starting to have those conversations about 'do we stay on AMP?'. It's obviously a difficult thing from a technical perspective, having to maintain that kind of infrastructure. But it's been really beneficial for us as well to kind of have these really performant pages – it's still something like 70% of all the content in top stories is our AMP pages.

Some publishers that have taken the leap and come off. And they've been very open about describing their experiences of doing that, which is invaluable for other publishers

Occasionally Google or Facebook will attend sessions with the group. As publishers, we don't often have the opportunity to put relevant questions directly to the platforms, so these meetings can be invaluable.

# From in-house, to agency, then going it alone, through to an acquisition – here's to 15 years' learning in SEO

## STEVEN VAN VESSUM

### DIRECTOR OF SEO, CONDUCTOR

---

Steven was always interested in trying out and breaking things – that's why his career has quickly taken him from the bottom to the top, from in-house, to agency, to opening his own, then pivoting to a SaaS solution, ContentKing. The company has recently been acquired by Conductor.

---

Even before I started studying IT at university, I was always fiddling around with computers, fixing people's computers, printers, networks. And then people started asking questions like, 'hey, can you build me a website?'. So I kind of went from there, and started getting better and better at building websites. Then people started asking, 'okay, Google seems pretty important – can you help me improve my visibility?'. And that's when I really started diving in and learning everything about it, reading up on all of the resources I could find, videos and such. I think that was 2005. A long time ago. But I really started to go down the rabbit hole in 2007. So it's been 15 years.

What's been good for me is transitioning through different roles. I started in-house in 2006 and went agency-side in 2009, but I got bored after a year. I thought I could do better. So I founded my own agency, together with my current business partner. I was picking up a lot of new skills on the way, because you have to, and we grew the agency to around 15 people. But we knew, if we were going to keep growing, it would be tough. It would take a whole different skill set, a different team, and so we decided we didn't want to go down that route. Instead, we had a great idea for a software platform. So we thought, 'okay, this is our moment to pivot away from the agency into the SEO-platform space'.

We ran the agency until 2015, when we then transitioned into ContentKing, and as we did that, we had to reinvent ourselves again. At the agency, we were good at building software and consulting on SEO, but building a SaaS business was wildly different. For me personally, doing digital marketing and SEO for a SaaS solution was wildly different from what I have been doing. As an agency, you're a consultant, you advise your clients on what they should and shouldn't do.

But now, at ContentKing, I was putting in all the work myself, I was coming up with new strategies for promoting content and I was implementing them. I was basically eating my own dog food – implementing all the stuff that I used to tell my clients. And some of it didn't work as well as I thought it would, for us at least. This space is a super-competitive one, because you're not only competing with other SEO platforms, there's also lots of agencies that are creating great content.

Looking back at the last couple of years, the biggest challenge for me has been competing with companies that have been around for 10 to 15 years longer than us. Much bigger sites, much more authority and much bigger teams. So it's kind of a 'David and Goliath' story. We really had to be smart about how we spend our time, looking for content gaps, topics that others hadn't really covered. And we would own that topic and take it from there. Often, you'll find adjacent topics that are equally interesting as the one you may have wanted to go for and haven't been covered by others properly. Going head-to-head, as a small brand, with limited budgets, a small team and limited authority as well, it's not usually a smart move. You need to have results, fast, as a growing company, because obviously you need to make money. So you've got to be smart. You've got to pick the battles you can win.

A lot of people that run an agency won't make the leap to building a software platform, for various reasons. There's a lot of people that do it, and it doesn't really work out. So part luck, part skill. What I'd say was essential to our success, besides a great team, was having a great business partner, who you're complementary to. My business partner and I are very different. He has certain skills I do not have, we have a different focus, and it's a very strong combination. So I think that's what's really helped us get to where we are right now.

Going through these different roles has kept SEO interesting for me. I had to relearn a lot of stuff and learn new things. It's definitely been a very interesting learning experience. But the SEO space is a tricky one, because basically everyone can call themselves an 'SEO expert'. It's not a protected profession. Today at ContentKing, we get around a million visits a year through our content-marketing and SEO efforts. Obviously people can give our software a try. But a lot of people are coming to us to educate themselves on SEO.

Sharing expertise through content

There's a lot of outdated and, frankly, bad advice out there. You can find anything you want online about SEO, to help you level up. But there's no 'SEO school', really. It's not like you can go to university and follow a four-year track. And to become a well-rounded SEO, a lot of this is about putting things in practice, trying things, breaking sites and trying to break Google, or to trick it into thinking something, to push the boundaries.

So I set out to change some of that, to contribute to the community-learning experience. That's why we created the ContentKing Academy, which I would say has been our marketing team's biggest success. We've had it now for four or five years and we've had millions of visitors. To me, that's mind-boggling. Because that means a lot of people could have picked up some really interesting ideas through reading our content. And that feels like a beautiful contribution to be able to make to improving the community.

We basically just collect all of our articles on the site – but we back up everything we write about SEO with sources and data where we can, and if it's anecdotal, or based on experience, we mention that too. We try to provide guardrails for people. And we try to make it as easy as possible to understand.

Google often puts out documentation for things like how they evaluate content, how crawling, indexing works, whatever, but a lot of their writing is quite technical. And you read it, and it raises all kinds of questions. Perhaps that's because at the end of the day, Google isn't making their money with the organic search results, they're making most of their money with PPC, having people buy ads. So they have conflicting motivations. But that means I don't think they have the SEOs', or even always the searchers' experience, in mind.

A lot of our content goes over their content and tries to explain it in a language that people actually understand. And we add examples. And we make everything very explicit. And sometimes there's just information missing in Google articles that we piece together. That's how we try to provide valuable content to the community. Of course, at the same time, we had to make sure the site was good for our company. It's always been a balancing act. The site has also served the company well, from a commercial point of view, and a branding perspective.

## Managing SEO through an acquisition

ContentKing has recently been acquired, so I'm going to have a very similar job to what I do now, just for a different company. So we're working on wrapping everything up and we're in the process of merging the companies so soon we'll really become part of Conductor. We're going from a three-person marketing team to like a 20-person marketing team. That's going to be a change. But I think I'll be given the opportunity to learn a lot of new things. Different people, new people, a bigger organisation, a more mature organisation. So I'm going to be doing a lot of learning. But I'm also going to be doing a lot of teaching, because a lot of the things that we learned over the last couple of years, that's enabled us to become successful as a small company, is very interesting to share with large organisations. So it goes both ways.

Having been acquired a few months ago, migrating things over is going to be my first project. That's going to be an interesting one, because we have two very authoritative sites, from an SEO point of view, a lot of organic traffic, and you want to combine that without giving up a big chunk of that. Or turning it into Frankenstein's monster. We're going to be looking at what pieces overlap – should we merge those articles? Should we just toss one? How can we hold on to all of our rankings as best we can? And keep providing users with a good user experience?

A couple of years ago at ContentKing, we had localised sites – in Dutch, Czech, French and Spanish. And we folded those into our English one, and so I now have a step-by-step process for managing web migrations, to prevent traffic losses. In this case, we have two live sites. And so first we need to do content inventory, for both, to understand what kind of topics are covered. Then we'll need to apply some kind of grading to try to understand, 'which articles are better? And is there anything that is not covered?'.

If you have two that cover similar areas and decide to go with the article that you deem better, it could be that the lesser article does cover some interesting stuff. So here you need not only to look at the content quality and the degree to which it satisfies user intent, and answers users' questions, but you also need to look at the keywords, the queries that both articles are relevant for and use all of the good bits from the lesser article, and all of the insights you can reuse. You should basically leverage that. It's basically about looking at what kind of content we have and how we can combine it to provide the best possible content for our audience.

I would like to see less crappy content out there. If there was a way it could be made clear to people what content they can trust, what content they can't trust, that would be great. Also, maybe a better way to debunk myths. For example, Moz is a well-known SEO platform. They created a metric, called Domain Authority. And it's meant to indicate some kind of authority about a website. But a lot of people don't understand the metric. And they will use the term, but they will use it incorrectly. And the same goes for a lot of other things. So knowing what content explains things well is really helpful. Because, in a lot of cases, experienced SEOs spend a lot of time helping people unlearn some of the stuff they learned, bad habits. So that's something I'd like to help change moving forwards.

# Understanding the Google SERP

## FELIX WELCKENBACH

### DIRECTOR INBOUND MARKETING, HOMETOGO

---

Felix has more than a decade of international-marketing expertise focussed on growing digital businesses. He started his SEO journey working at online-dating platform Parship before progressing to senior roles at live-entertainment company Eventim and travel brand Expedia. He's been in-house, worked as a consultant and currently leads inbound marketing at Berlin-based vacation rental marketplace HomeToGo, where he and his team look after SEO, PR, brand-building and social media.

---

At HomeToGo, our concept of 'inbound marketing' has been a strong driver behind the success of organic growth. It has meant combining SEO, PR, social media and brand-building under one umbrella, including engineering teams and data analysts, aligned by a common set of OKRs (Objectives and Key Results).

HomeToGo has been going through tremendous growth and change in recent years. What started as a 'meta search' for vacation rentals, working with thousands of partners, is, since last September, a public company. And we're evolving into a fully-integrated marketplace and Online Travel Agency (OTA), meaning our team set-up was in need of a brush-up.

Essentially, we've enabled each team in inbound to increase their focus by dividing them into functional groups. That's because firstly, after multiple acquisitions, we wanted each team to be able to handle more scope, while continuing to push the boundaries on innovation and performance. Secondly, being a public company meant new requirements for our communication teams, which is now focussed on corporate, employer branding and investor relations, on top of consumer communications. Last but not least, we needed to keep up with the speed at which Google and the search landscape evolves, and the increasing amount of complexity that creates for our teams.

In parallel, we introduced the concept of 'product ownership' on the SEO team, giving people end-to-end responsibility for researching, scoping and prioritising user (human and bot) problems that have a meaningful business impact and help us deliver on our OKRs. This role is predominantly owned by the business part of the team, while technical teams focus on investigating, implementing and maintaining scalable technical solutions that help deliver on our OKRs. Similarly, our engineers own all aspects of shipping an initiative from investigation to implementation, along with QA and tech documentation. This way, we create a product-led operating model, leading to more scalability and the ability to deliver results with an ever-increasing scope.

A positive side-effect of allowing team members to play to their individual strengths, and double-down on what they like and are good at, is we have opened up new career paths. This creates long-term opportunities and aspirations within the team, all allowing us to stay ahead of the curve.

Equipped with the right focus and team set-up, we saw the need to come up with a scalable, programmatic solution for optimising our assets, allowing us to identify, forecast and capitalise on the biggest opportunities across our vast range of domains. This is where Google SERP data comes into play.

## Understanding the SERP

Travel is a unique industry – not only because it's super competitive – but because your partners are sometimes your biggest competitors. This is no more true than of Google itself, which has dramatically increased the share of space it gives to its own products in the SERP in recent years. The most prominent in travel are the Google Hotel Finder and Google Vacation Rental Finder, and this ultimately pushes organic results further down the page. On top of this, Google has been experimenting with changing the number of search results that appear on each page, going from 10 down to seven or eight sometimes.

Since Google introduced these bespoke SERP features, we have noticed that, despite our rankings improving, our click-through rate (CTR) has not. In fact, it has consistently dropped year on year. On top of that, for most travel companies, Google is still the most important customer-acquisition channel. The industry is dependent on Google, spending billions on ads every year, while being squeezed in organic search results at the same time. Because of this, we've been quite vocal, along with other companies, about what we see as Google's self-preferential treatment and have advocated for there to be a level playing field, so it's a fair competition.

In the meantime, with organic space shrinking, yet our competition increasing and investors expecting further organic growth – we were really wondering what approach we should take. To try to deal with this at HomeToGo, what started as an ad-hoc analysis of the SERP resulted in a large project where we started sourcing SERP data more programmatically and combining it with other data sources. We quickly noticed the value in the information. On top of getting CTR curves, what data source, other than Google itself, could be better-suited to trying to understand search intent, related topics, FAQs and more?

When we dug deeper into bespoke CTR analysis, and compared keywords that triggered SERP-features against those that did not, CTR curves were substantially worse. No surprise here. The 'above-the-fold' Google widget catches attention, and takes clicks away from organic results, even though we question whether the UX and limited choice of options offered are really better than services found below.

Initially, understanding what was happening in the SERP really helped with our internal communication. Both for setting expectations, as well as for explaining performance trends and answering questions like 'if our average rank is getting better, why are we getting less traffic?'.

# Using SERP data to our advantage

We have more recently started to use this SERP data to come up with actionable insights that we can use to optimise our processes and identify new opportunities. Over the years, we have put together a comprehensive database of thousands of destination and travel-topic queries, so we can better understand the demand side of our marketplace.

We know that searchers' behaviour changes over time, often due to external things like the COVID-19 pandemic, new competitors or trends like 'workations'. Google is constantly adapting to this changing behaviour and trying to match searchers' intent with the most relevant results – so we have to keep our databases up-to-date too.

When trying to automate the update process we ran into some issues. For example, by checking search volume for query combinations like 'destination + accommodation type' we found some interesting outliers that needed manual attention. The most notable was probably 'Tokio Hotel', because, although Tokyo is a popular destination, it turns out, the band of the same name is even more so.

This is where SERP data comes in handy. We needed a programmatic way to identify searchers' intent. Instead of relying on industry tool data or manual checks, what better source to use than Google, which spends millions on getting intent right?

Data providers like DataForSEO, SERP API and others give you a snapshot of the SERP for a given keyword. With this as the starting point, we've kicked-off a project to classify the SERP for our most important destination queries by looking at the SERP composition, and how many travel versus non-travel sites would rank. In the 'Tokio Hotel' example, rankings of editorial sites like Rolling Stone indicate users might mean something else other than finding a hotel in Tokyo.

Another example was the core update in June 2021 where our US site lost around 50% of its visibility. Among other reasons, we found that we had lost rankings for ambiguous terms, like 'apartment rental' and 'house rental', where it's not clear what the intent is. It could be short-term rentals – our expertise – or long-term rentals, so finding an apartment or house to live in. By looking at the SERP again, we found that the share of travel sites ranking for these terms decreased and more real-estate sites moved into the top 10. A valuable insight, as it's helping us to re-prioritise our target queries, not only by search volume, but also by target intent.

I'm also a big believer in the value of Google Autocomplete. When you type 'cottages in Cornwall' into Google, you'll get suggestions like 'cottages in Cornwall that are dog-friendly' or 'cottages in Cornwall with a hot tub and sea view'. Google doesn't give you exact numbers here, but often these long-tail queries are missing from the industry tools and do not come up during classic keyword research.

To drive growth in an environment of shrinking organic space, Google SERP data has provided some valuable and actionable insights for us.

# Whether it's Panda, a pandemic or pregnancy – you've got to get used to change

## AMANDA WHITE
### FREELANCE CONSULTANT, AMANDA WHITE DIGITAL

Amanda's passion for photography helped her get her first break in SEO. Since then, she's worked both agency-side and in-house, with big British brands like Argos and Furniture World. The pandemic finally nudged her to go freelance, meaning she's often working part-time, in-house, and for people who hadn't really heard of SEO until their business was forced online.

Going right back to school, I loved IT. I did it at A Level and it was just one of those things where I thought 'I want to get involved in this. I want to know what's going on'. I also studied photography at college, then university, and ended up with a job at a photography processing shop, and it was great. But, moving on from a photography degree, I lost the passion. I just didn't want to pick up my camera anymore.

Fortunately, the shop also had a website, and they said, 'if you're interested, you can start learning a bit about that'. So I began creating a few simple banners using Photoshop, which I knew from my course. The next question, obviously, was, 'well... how can we get found on Google?'. That's where I started to get that 'little itch' for SEO.

I then applied for an agency role, which I didn't get, but they said that I had a lot of passion and I just needed to sort of 'swot up' on SEO. So I spent the next six months learning it. Then eventually they were recruiting again and this time I got the job. That was 2010.

## From building backlinks to building a career

With SEO, there is no official career path. If you want to be a doctor, you know what you have to do. You have to study the exact medical science. There's a specific way of treating people. It's regulated. It's organised.

Whereas SEO isn't really like that. There's so many people selling 'snake oil'. You'll often pick up clients where they've been sold 'SEO'. But they've basically just been given a report each month, and the company doesn't actually do anything.

I started in link building and got massively thrown in at the deep end working for Argos, The Range, Homebase, some really big brands. That progressed into technical SEO and SEO audits – it all got quite in-depth, quite quickly, and I really enjoyed that.

But, just after – Google released the Panda update – and it was panic stations. Our industry, our SEO methods, were based on building backlinks, on building content, and suddenly it was like the whole internet was affected.

There were some really big companies that were heavily buying backlinks, using some unsavoury tactics of over-building links, or using too much of the same anchor text. And they were taken down overnight by Google, to set an example. This put the fear into SEOs. The way it had worked had changed – and the way we were doing things had to change.

At first, it was like, 'oh my goodness, what am I going to do? I'm not going to have a job. SEO is dead', which I know now you hear all the time. Then you realise, 'well, actually, no, there are ways to help people here'. It's about how you evolve. And all of that propelled me on in my career.

Previously, it could be seen as 'whoever has the deepest pockets', because whoever could buy the most links on the most authoritative sites would be the ones that ranked higher. You would find small websites just popping up out of nowhere, and dominating the search results and taking that competition.

Of course, there is still an element of big brands having bigger budgets for advertising, but now there is a much more level playing field. Even if you're a really small, niche brand, and you're selling something quite different, if you are providing content that helps people, they will find it, and you will get surfaced in your own right.

The thing with Google is, it is a brand, itself. They are not going to want to give somebody a search result page where they land and go, 'oh, this result is rubbish'. They don't want to provide a bad customer service either. So we had to become more creative. We had to produce something that was useful to the customer. With Argos, we went down the route of creating 'buyers guides', with the aim of helping people, creating content that would naturally get shared, whether it was video content or images or infographics.

Actually, I realised, the industry wasn't giving people value before. Yes, it boosted the rankings, to therefore bring the revenue. But we weren't thinking about the customer – no one was going to follow that link into that website. Now it is much more customer focused. For me – this all comes down to a 'common-sense' approach.

In my in-house role at Furniture World, when I joined, they had the furniture website, but they also had a subsidiary website just selling oak furniture. It was non-transactional. It was not found. It was not doing anything. Over the years of working there, working on their content, working on the keywords, and making sure everything was aligned, we made that hugely successful in terms of revenue.

It got to the point where we actually migrated it, because we could just use the content and structure to boost the main site. We eventually killed off the oak furniture website, which is quite cool in some respects, because it went from nothing, to everything, to being migrated. It's like the full journey.

One of the main things here was about educating the organisation – they would use industry or suppliers' terminology on their customer facing website – so would call a wardrobe a 'robe', because that's how they would order them in. I was having to explain 'well actually to a customer a "robe" is a dressing gown'. So we had to do a lot of work around keyword research to get all the right terms – and that was a huge win for that website.

You also want to know what products are coming in, in the future, because you want to start creating those pages ready for when the stock arrives. So you need to be speaking to internal-buying teams. And they might not want to give you that information. Equally, you need to get developers on side too, whether they prefer tickets on JIRA or face-to-face calls where you actually explain what the problem is.

A lot of people think that in in-house SEO, you're kind of in silo, because other people don't understand the job. But actually, you're leaning on all the people around you. I think it's vital for the role to work.

## A personal and professional transition

If you had spoken to me five years ago, and asked, 'would you ever be freelance?', I would have said 'not at all, not a chance'. I did not have that confidence, and I was more than happy being in a team, reporting to somebody else. But I think, a combination of becoming a mum and the pandemic, it made me realise that life is short. If you want to do something, you just have to crack on and do it.

Today a lot of my clients are small to medium-sized businesses – where often I fit in as part of their team when they haven't hired a full-time, in-house person. I think the pandemic has obviously, massively pushed a lot more people online. There were so many brick-and-mortar-only stores that literally had to get online overnight.

So now, there's a whole flood of people that have never had SEO before, never really thought about SEO, don't even know what SEO is. And they suddenly want to get online. They don't want to employ a full-time person in-house, so they might scratch the surface with a freelancer and start to see the benefits. Then perhaps upscale.

I currently work with a physiotherapist and a sales presentation trainer. They didn't really have websites, or they weren't using their websites – they were word of mouth. Then suddenly it was Zoom meetings, or Zoom training, and everybody was looking for the people offering that instead. People with a physical service were suddenly left high and dry.

Again, for me, it's the common-sense approach. With the physio, for example, he wanted to be found for osteopathy services and soft-tissue massage, but had changed the names of the products to something that he thought was quite creative. But nobody's searching for that.

He was burying the most important pages. So it was about simplifying it to say 'they've got a problem, they need their problem fixed'. And one of those things they're going to want to know is 'how can you fix me? And how much is it going to cost?'. So it's bringing what the customer needs to the forefront.

Sometimes people might think 'SEO, I don't know what that is, but my website, I understand that'. But you have to be quite clear – SEO really is your website – to a large extent. And a lot of that can be backed up by keyword search volumes.

For SMEs, it is mainly about budget. And, for a lot of them, they can make huge gains with their content. It's lovely to know that you're helping people – some of the reviews I've had are just insane – people saying they were scared of SEO and I've just made it so much more accessible to them. When they see the gains that are possible, it's no longer this 'taboo subject' where it's all, you know, dodgy buying backlinks, or a sort of shady industry. And that reputation is still part of the challenge.

Compared to a decade ago, the thing that now keeps me in SEO is the constant change. You're still playing a game, but it's just a different version each year. Or, not even each year, every five minutes, sometimes. Now, Google announces they do at least 200 algorithm changes a year.

So, there's a lot going on, but, now they maybe do a little tweaking, something that maybe affects one small area of the industry. Still, the end goal is to get more traffic and to get more revenue for the client. I think if you don't like change, don't get involved. I've worked with some people, even to some extent myself when things changed the first time, that got scared. But if you are up for constantly learning and growing, I definitely think it's a career worth exploring.

For me personally, because I had my little boy and I was away from the scene for a bit, I had to come back in again, where I felt a little like 'I'm out of my depth, things have moved on, algorithms have changed, I'm not up to speed'. So I got stuck into courses and conferences, and groups like Women in Tech SEO. And that shows other people and clients that I am keeping up, even though there isn't an 'official' path to go down.

Professionally, for me, bringing it back to basics – aligning the keyword with what you want to be found for – is my number one SEO recommendation. Personally, the pandemic gave me the time to reevaluate what I wanted to do in life, and perhaps working for myself was a much better idea.

# Edge is the next frontier in SEO – here's where to begin

## NICK WILSDON
### FOUNDER AND CEO, TORQUE

Nick has spent more than two decades in digital marketing – which began in earnest when he started talking to a Russian woman online, went out there to meet her, then decided to set up his life there. After launching a number of successful businesses, and accidentally attracting the attention of authorities, the couple eventually made their way back to the UK. He's consulted for Vodafone and eBay, and founded consultancy firm Torque in 2020. Because his family speaks Russian, they've just welcomed a Ukrainian family into their home.

I always wanted to understand how things work and to discover new frontiers. And even after 22 years working in SEO, I still haven't lost that feeling. Every time I think we're plateauing, new areas open up and the whole industry forks or pivots. And at the moment for me, that's about edge computing.

If I was an in-house technical SEO right now, I would be looking at this area very closely, because it's going to be hugely influential, especially at the large enterprise level. In fact, I think it'll be vital for all SEOs to have some understanding of it. Because the edge is hugely powerful, there's huge capability in it and what it can do at scale is phenomenal.

For SEOs, it's going to help you with rolling out SEO proof-of-concept plans and programmes. But there's huge interest from CFOs, because if they can see that an edge team can make things work in weeks, instead of months, or even years, that's massively beneficial. It allows companies to move at a faster pace. Velocity is something that every large company is really focusing on at the moment. Test it, work it, move quicker, be more agile. Edge is definitely a way you can do that.

To explain edge computing: we have content delivery networks (CDNs), and these are networks of hundreds of thousands of servers positioned all around the world. Companies like Akamai, Cloudflare and Fastly own them, and they can essentially help you localise certain tasks to where webpage requests are made, to save trips back to your origin server and therefore, processing power. So if I've got a server in London, and I want a user to interact with a webpage in Mumbai, then I don't want them to request the webpage all the way from London. It doesn't make sense, there's latency involved. What I want to do is have an almost 'cached 'version of the webpage that exists on a server there. And we call this 'the edge'.

Previously we just used the edge to serve content through that network. But it's become a lot more advanced, what we now call 'edge compute'. There's increased processing power in the servers, to the degree that we can run scripts on the edge, run code. We can store data in these places, and we synchronise all of that globally, as we used to synchronise everything for CDNs. So this has kind of opened up the whole frontier.

## Redirects on the edge

Page redirects are a really good use case. Essentially, the internet is a whole series of webpages and these pages move all the time. A large job for SEOs is managing what happens when webpages move, what they're redirected to, and making sure that Google understands that the webpage has moved so it can reindex it and put it back into its results.

Now, if you imagine when you go to a website, you may go to a certain URL and you get redirected to the next one. The way that'll work in computing terms is, I will come in through a CDN, through Akamai, for example, I'll touch on the edge, I'll then go to the webpage I've requested, to the origin page. Now, we can have a cached page there, but if the page itself is a redirect, then we're going to go to the origin, we're then going to find out on the origin that we actually meant to go to another page, and we'll then get redirected out. And then we'll come back in again through the CDN and go to the page that we're meant to go to.

Redirects are very costly in terms of those kinds of trips. They have a huge overhead. So if we can redirect the user on the edge, we can just find out where they're meant to have gone when they first touched the edge and we can send them immediately to that final point. It's a really simple use case, but this is why I believe all redirects should be done on the edge. It's great for users, because this means faster webpages. So say you normally access a webpage in – time to first byte – 700 milliseconds. Using the edge for redirects, you would then access this in, say, 250 milliseconds. It's great for Google because it likes fast sites, and it's great at an enterprise level, because you're reducing the impact on the origin server by putting all this heavy redirection load onto the edge. For one of my clients, I'm redirecting over a billion requests a month and on some pages, we've had a 30% improvement in webpage-response time – 64% is the maximum improvement we've had, just by cutting out these jumps.

## Managing bots, A/B testing and storage

As a technical SEO, a lot of time is spent trying to work out 'what do you want Googlebot to crawl?'. But on some sites, you have many different parameters for each individual webpage, so if you crawl a site, it may only have 20,000 'actual pages', but from an SEO point of view, we can find out it has 500,000. Say you have an ecommerce store, pages like myecommstore.com/dresses/black?var=size3 might all get crawled. Then extrapolate that onto the entire catalogue.

Of course, Google doesn't really want to be crawling hundreds of thousands of pages that aren't particularly useful, so you'll be wasting your 'crawl budget'. Crawl budget isn't a problem if you're a small site, or even a medium site, but certainly for large sites, it's something that has to be considered. That's just wasted computation. On edge, you can manage what bots consume, to help crawling become far more efficient. You might look at rewriting URLs, forward rewriting URLs and you can change how Google perceives URLs. Akamai and Cloudflare have talked about 'URL hygiene', and you can have rules that basically control how Googlebot and other bots are crawling website URLs.

Thinking about A/B testing, we've been working on one project where the company has a menu that only exists on the homepage, a big problem for SEOs, because we want the links, and everything else to go through the entire site. So you can create a test on the edge to make that menu persist on every page, to insert it dynamically and run A/B testing on it. The benefits of doing this on the edge are that you're working within the architecture of the brand. You haven't got to get some other third-party A/B testing tools, you can do this natively, with the architecture that's already paid for. It's also safe because you're doing all within the architecture of the brand itself, especially good for large enterprises because they may feel very nervous about running all their traffic through a third-party, A/B testing system. Also, adding it would require a million different development meetings, then the dev team would have to build it, which would take months. And we don't know it's even going to work. So what we want to do is quickly test it for a couple of months and see if it's better. It's something that I can get up and running in a few weeks. This is why enterprises are hiring edge teams, because we can test things very fast, roll them out and see if they work.

You might also want to sync some of your data with the edge, if it's data that can change the request. So say you want to do personalisation, you can synchronise data that tells you about someone, their preferences, their likes, and then manipulate the request as it goes through, using the edge.

It's a case of you trying to take some lightweight services and put them on the edge, to build layers on top of what you're doing, that massively improve the experience. What you're doing is alleviating the processing overhead on your origin server, but also, you're just making the whole thing faster for users. That's why one of the CDNs is called Fastly. CDNs are all about improving the experience for users. So if I can do some computation, run a script, where I can do a redirect, or I can do something at the edge, that means you don't have to take that long, costly journey all the way to the origin server.

With edge, there are lots of people debating how it should be used and whether it should be used. Edge computing isn't going to do the heavy, heavy lifting, it's not going to replace the cloud. And it's not going to replace large data banks of origin servers. I'm very keen not to move a load of problems onto the edge, you don't want to move all your tech debt onto the edge, where we fix it now, but we create a problem that someone else has to deal with in a few years. So I'm always looking for ways of fixing things that are better, sort of more long-term solutions. And that comes back to my experience of enterprise and large companies, that you have to do things right, really, or it will come back to haunt you in a few years.

## Using the edge to save the planet

Digital emissions are comparable to the aviation industry, which is quite shocking to me, and that's because we do things like running all these computers and servers, with robots checking all these huge sites all day long. On the edge, we can do things to control those bots, control the crawl, and drastically reduce things like the number of redirects, those backwards and forward trips. This is all useless traffic. And that makes a real difference for large companies, because with very large websites, you're talking about billions, or tens of billions, of crawls per year. I know large companies who are now using computation costs and CPU cycles as one of their main KPIs in this area, which is a very progressive way to think about it. Making changes like this can offer a definite CPU saving, which is a monetary saving, but also a planetary saving as well.

Google and a lot of the search engines are also very concerned with making those processes more efficient, not least because it's good for the planet. They are already trying very hard to talk to SEOs about performance – anything we do in terms of making our pages more lightweight and more efficient, improving page-speed performance, page-speed loading, requesting content faster, less demand on the server – is brilliant for users, but it's conveniently good for Google as well, because it's going to reduce their costs.

People are getting really excited about the edge now – you can learn how to use it in Fastly – they've got huge support for developers and learning. Cloudflare also offers many of their services free, which means it's incredibly accessible for a small website. It won't cost you anything to test and learn and run cloud services in it. So, the edge is good for users, companies, search engines – and it's definitely good for the planet, too – how can it not be the next frontier for SEO?

# SEO is more important than ever – and even after two decades on the frontline – it's always a learning curve

## STEVEN WILSON-BEALES
### HEAD OF SEO AND EDITORIAL PRODUCT, GLOBAL

---

Steve started out in editorial working at Universal Music and, after a stint managing content in education, found his way back into the music industry as Head of Internet at Ministry of Sound. After interviewing some of the biggest names in dance music, he went on to work for Microsoft as a Managing Editor for the MSN team. He then joined Global eight years ago, where his role now combines editorial, SEO and product. He also co-chairs the Journalism Advisory Board for the Association of Online Publishers.

---

I think it's safe to say that before 2017, most news publishers had become over-reliant on Facebook as their main driver of audience. But when conversations around #fakenews forced Facebook to reduce news-publisher visibility, attention quickly shifted to news SEO as the primary source of referral traffic. That's been my journey over the last five years – helping teams understand and optimise for search intent – and it's been quite an adventure.

Like any other publisher, search at Global is more important than it's ever been. I'm in the fortunate position of not only advising our teams on SEO but, as a product owner, directly shaping the Content Management System (CMS) that can deliver on that search excellence. So that's my role – real-time news planning and reaction, technical SEO product ownership and supporting multiple teams, from marketing, commercial to broadcasting.

I don't know if there's such a thing as a 'typical' lone in-house SEO, but if there is, I'm one of them. Today I have more than 10 different websites to look after and I can say with almost absolute confidence that no day is exactly the same. One day I might be running editorial training, or doing competitive keyword research or helping teams plan ahead for one of our big events like Capital's Summertime Ball. Then again, I might be running an SEO workshop with our charities team, advising on international SEO or supporting recruitment SEO. Each of these areas are very different, but that's the excitement of being an SEO – the chance to dive into completely new topics, markets and audiences.

## From radio broadcaster to global publisher

It's been quite a few years since Global was purely a radio company – we're now a media and entertainment group where digital plays a leading part in our growth. As an SEO, it's been really exciting to work with editorial teams to figure out the different ways we can optimise video and audio content to pull out the best bits for our audience – and for Google.

On a daily basis we will be interviewing any number of top celebrities and politicians, attending junkets or developing serious news investigations – and for each media asset delivered, we need to work out the best way of attracting traffic from search. Often, this comes down to making sure we have lots of supporting text for that asset, and helping teams understand what overarching topic this asset is part of, so we can frame the content accordingly.

Likewise, we also have to pay attention to copywriting outside of our own websites, which is why Youtube optimsation continues to be important for us. We've seen some fantastic viewing figures there, especially on brands like LBC, but we can never assume we will get those numbers, purely due to the nature of the video, it has to be supported by keyword research and copy layout. Considering the majority of videos featured in Google search are Youtube videos, I think it's safe to say Youtube SEO is not going away anytime soon.

But we're not just interested in extending our reach in search for 'reach's sake'. In recent years, we've really focused attention on our Global Player app, which offers everything from live and catch up radio, playlists, podcasts and video. It's been interesting to work in this space as an SEO because we're really focused on driving 'conversion', in this case, app registrations. That's why we're thinking a lot more now about product-led SEO. Yes, we want to create great pages that answer that search query, but we also want to ensure that the audience stays once they arrive. So the question is – how can we attract more invested consumers through search, as opposed to casual users swiping through their social media newsfeed?

## Global and news SEO

Like any publisher, we want to be first in search with our news stories – and that means looking at a whole host of things that might be a little different from traditional SEO. What hasn't changed is the absolute need for regularly checking the actual search results pages for changes.

There are a lot of amazing SEO tools out there, but you also need to be looking at the SERPs and spotting the clues. What pages are currently ranking in Top Stories? What angles, language and formats are they using? What's the volume of articles on that topic? Can we compete? Is it worth targeting your editorial team to try? And of course, technical SEO has become a much bigger deal with Core Web Vitals, forcing us to look more closely at how the content is being delivered. In short, there's a lot more for SEOs to consider.

With so many newsrooms competing for the same story and knowing a news story might only have a short-life span of two to three days, we've taken a renewed focus on 'evergreen' and news-explainer articles. These have a tendency to stick around a lot longer in the SERPs, if you've answered all the key user questions, of course. Saying that, it's no easy task to ask editors to shift attention to evergreens when we can still see tremendous traffic spikes from daily news stories.

So, one top tip I have is, if you're trying to influence an editorial team to produce more evergreen content, or anything search-related for that matter, always make sure you have one or two examples where the method has been a success. That can be from your own website or elsewhere, no matter how small. If it's good evidence, then it should be a no-brainer for editorial teams to go ahead and execute.

# A punt on Core Web Vitals

We started the work on Core Web Vitals about a year and a half ago – and that was definitely a learning curve for me – and meant that I had to work much more closely with our development teams. But the work has been hugely successful and we've now got some of the fastest news websites in the UK.

This has also been a process of education for the whole SEO industry, too, not least because we had mixed messages from Google about the importance of addressing Core Web Vitals. On the one hand, it was being flagged as absolutely necessary, but it was then difficult to pinpoint the precise impact of doing the work.

I think we did a good job at Global because with Core Web Vitals the aims of the SEO and the development team are one and the same – we all want to create fast, smoother loading websites with great UX for our users. And what we're seeing now is that competitor websites that haven't done any of that work are seeing a decline in rankings. This kind of technical SEO has been really rewarding for me – I have a better understanding of how developers work and I know that if I want to influence decisions there I have to be part of their workflows.

Going forward, publishers will need to invest more in SEO that supports their editorial teams, because the landscape has become so much more nuanced. One of the challenges is that, traditionally, you simply gave editorial teams some SEO copywriting training and expected them to get the results. And that's not the case anymore. It's much tougher out there in the search results and Google is releasing many more core updates at a faster rate.

So you need experts, feeding back to editorial teams and saying, 'this has changed, we now need to write in a different way'. You need dedicated teams, SEO editors, working with journalists, really, to get the results. You need writers to write the stories, then you need SEO teams to advise on how to optimise them.

One way to tackle this might be to identify 'SEO champions', which we have at Global. We've identified those writers that are super passionate about search and have been working with these advocates to share lessons across the wider team. This often leads to new or improved search-optimised features, which are delivering some wonderful results.

## Some SEO tip for beginners

One handy tip, particularly for a beginner in-house SEOs, is that you might spot lots of different things that are wrong on a website. And you might want to just plough in and fix all those things.

But I think it's important to take a step back and really think about how you're going to report it and measure it. Because if you plough in and fix many different things, it may be difficult to pinpoint exactly what you did that led to that result.

I've certainly done that myself, where I've gone 'right, I'm going to fix this, this, this, that' and we've seen an uplift. And then I think, 'oh no, if I had been able to demonstrate the method and the success of that, I could have used that as a really successful case study to help me in other projects'.

I've also done a lot of work in educating the teams at Global about how driving traffic from search is never about just doing one thing - it's usually a suite of things we need to do. In a way, SEO is a bit like problem solving using a swiss army knife of ideas.

It's always useful to have a mental checklist of all the different things that you need to go through when trying to address a search issue. And that checklist needs to include both the very simple things you could easily overlook as well as the advanced. I've seen plenty of cases when major SEO issues have been caused by a simple line of code, or an incorrect submission to Google Search Console. So think BIG but also very, very, SMALL.

Saying that, sometimes the challenge could be of a completely different nature. Maybe you're seeing a bigger search challenge because the competition has simply increased the size of their editorial team, or hired additional SEOs. Which makes my role all the more exciting.

# The future of SEO – including pre-rendering success

## EMIRHAN YASDIMAN

### GLOBAL SEO LEAD, METRO AG

Emirhan started his working life as a data analyst in Turkey in 2008.
The company was majority offline, but as the youngest person in his
team, he eventually found himself building their website, along with
a sophisticated database. This is where he discovered SEO. He went
on to work at the first SEO agency in Turkey, at the birth of search
marketing here, and worked his way up to managing and growing
teams at different companies. After the coup attempt in 2016, Emirhan
secured a role at Trivago in Germany and moved his family here. He's
been at Metro AG, the German multinational wholesaler, for three years.

Metro operates in 25 countries and employs around 100,000 people worldwide. So it's a big company.

They focus on B2B wholesale for hotels, restaurants, catering companies, mostly selling food and food-related equipment, so you can choose from 300 different sorts of ovens, for example. If we find things that have a 200 or 300 search volume, that's great, because not many people search for 'how to calculate breakfasts per person'. You have to find niche things like this and rank on them.

Metro never had an SEO before I joined in 2019. They have blogs, they have pages, everything, but they never cared too much about organic traffic. They also never had a centrally managed online-marketing team before. Every country is its own company, has its own CEO and structure, some of them employed a couple of people in SEO, sometimes they worked with agencies. But there was nowhere to aggregate that experience if someone was doing amazingly well. So it's part of my job to assist those countries to get to the next level on performance marketing and SEO.

I was initially hired for a subsidiary of Metro, Metro Markets, which handles the ecommerce business – and was only launched itself in 2019. When I joined, there was no website, but now we live in Spain and Italy is next. The company quickly realised, 'okay, this is working. Let's do it for the whole group'. So I now have two teams, two people in Metro Markets working only on ecommerce, and three people in Metro AG, working for the whole group.

## A pre-rendering solution

My biggest success to date is the work done on the marketplace. We started from zero, there was nothing, no shop, and we went to 12,000 page-one rankings in one year, then 27,000 in two years. Now we have 272,000 in three years. And that's only for Germany. So it has gone really well. I cannot tell you 'I did this and we had these 200,000 rankings', it's the accumulation of hundreds of initiatives. But one thing that was definitely a great decision was building our own pre-rendering tool.

We have our own CMS, our own ecommerce platform, everything that we use for our marketplace is developed in-house. It's good and bad. It means everything that we have is kind of 'mid-level', not the best of the best, but we can play around with everything. However, because we use a customised Angular framework, it isn't a fast website, and we're also using JavaScript.

Before we developed the tool, we already knew there was only a certain amount of time, or let's say money, that Google was going to spend trying to understand our web pages. If there's a product page, they just want to delete all the boilerplate stuff and take the product information, and the image. If they don't do this cleaning, or 'rendering', they will waste a lot of server space.

When you have a JavaScript website, this rendering can take a lot of processing power. So we knew Google was only going to render the pages that were important enough for them – but there's no interface that tells you which pages those are, and therefore those that are indexed, by Google. We were using a third-party tool, which was rendering our pages, but it wasn't doing it correctly. And this was critical.

As an ecommerce company, we use Google Shopping ads, and what this means is, you give Google a feed of this information, and then they check your webpage, to see if you're offering the same prices that you advertise. So if you're advertising something for €200, and you have €210 on the page, then you get banned. The problem with the third-party solution was that it wasn't updating quickly enough. So if we changed the price on the website, the pre-rendered version of the same page was not changing fast enough. So, when Google comes, I'm showing it the old page, and I actually now have the higher price on the page, which was creating a problem.

Instead, we said 'okay, can we do this ourselves?', because we were also wasting a lot of resources in the process. Our solution, put simply, was just to give the search engines properly pre-rendered pages – and we did that by turning it into HTML, then delivering this to Google and Bing.

Anyone else visiting the website, they would get the usual content, the JavaScript, so nothing changes for users.

Today, we have around 500,000 products in the marketplace and we have around 70,000 or 80,000 non-indexed pages, always, because they are new pages and it takes time for Google to index everything. But that means we have more than 400,000 pages that are indexed. That was it – you have to get the page indexed for it to rank – that was the first step.

We know that today Amazon delivers everyone, search engine or human, the HTML page – so they don't need to do anything specific for Google bot. That's what we are trying to do next, to bring pre-rendering to users too, so we don't need to do anything specific for search engines, we will serve them what we serve to everyone.

## Getting influence – and becoming cross-functional

The biggest challenge I have today is making sure I have influence in the group. We already know the management respects our expertise – because we always back our claims with data or experience. But today I work with five to seven different product teams. And, when you're starting out, and they don't know you, it takes a lot of work to, for example, convince them that, if they spent three sprints working on a feature you want, they will get more traffic, revenue, or sessions, or some other KPI they're measuring. It's good that I've come from an agency, because there, you have seven or eight clients at a time, so in a way I can just treat them as separate clients. But getting this influence can be hard to find your way around.

It's all about establishing trust and getting to know enough people who actually recognise you as someone who does what they say they're going to do. In my team, what we try to do is, every time a product team does something for us, in three months or so, we give them feedback.

We may say, 'since you did this in December, we have, month-on-month, this much more revenue, thanks to your work'. So they understand why we did something and how well it worked. If it doesn't work, we also tell them, as there are never any guarantees. But at least we can say, 'this was the thought process. And this is how it panned out. And that's the reason'. Of course, if this happens five out of five times, they will stop prioritising your work. If this happens, one out of nine, they also say, 'okay, don't worry about it'.

In terms of centralising the online-marketing operation, doing something like this is all about the people, too. In the first meeting, you have to be smiling, you have to be positive. You don't want to be saying, 'okay, this is what we're going to do now and I will tell you what to do'. That doesn't work. And first, you need to ask questions, things like 'do you work with an agency? How much do you spend on SEO? How can we help you reduce that? Or spend it more efficiently?'. If you spent €40,000 per year on an agency, and then you didn't need to do it anymore, that's €40,000 more in your marketing budget. Who doesn't like that? Every CEO and CMO loves the idea of not having to spend a certain budget for SEO. At Metro, we can now centrally create English content for our teams, all they need to do is translate it, or we can translate it for them, all they need to do is fix it later.

We all know digital marketing is getting more expensive every year. If you look at 10 years ago – a €25 cost-per-click (CPC) was an impossible thing, now it is not. So when summer comes, if you want to appear in search for 'hotels in Barcelona', you probably need to spend €15 to €20 per click, which is a lot of money. So I hope people will see the importance of SEO more and more.

Also, most companies don't know where to put SEO – should it be with the marketing team? Should it be with the product team? Should it be next to the developers? There is always this confusion. So I hope people will start having these cross-functional SEO teams. It may be you have three technical SEOs in product, one person working with the content team, then another two people working with the marketing team to do press releases and back-link building. But they are managed by one person. So it can influence the whole company.

We are at a point where your brand reputation can actually influence your organic traffic – the reviews you have on Google can even influence your organic traffic on non-branded terms. So SEO can now mean a lot of things. You may have an amazing website, it's fast, it has great content and everything – but if your warehouse and shipping sucks and people are leaving angry reviews, you will start losing traffic and you won't know why. Here, you're not ranking because you're bad at an operational level, it's nothing that you can affect, right? That's why I believe SEOs need to keep track of everything and really need to be informed about everything going on in the company.

I'd say it should always sit under marketing, because, by definition, it's a traffic channel – you are reporting a traffic revenue stream. But the people should work in a different way, because you cannot say, 'I am marketing, I didn't know product was working on that'. You don't have that luxury anymore.

# About Blue Array

We stand for SEO.

From the day we launched in early 2015, we've been pioneering a unique hybrid of agency and consultancy, we call this a 'consulgency'. It's an approach that allows us to give our clients the individual attention they need with the scale of an agency.

Never having taken investment, we have bootstrapped our way to over 50 employees, multi-million pounds of turnover, believing in SEO and its power to take businesses such as heycar, RAC and Pret to places they never thought possible.

We are an agency defining an industry, by putting purpose ahead of profit, turning obsession into drive, and using knowledge to educate.

Our mission is to elevate our people, customers and industry through SEO and use our business to positively influence a better world.

Find out more about us at bluearray.co.uk

**Simon Schnieders**
Founder

# Learn SEO the Blue Array Way

From building your skills to taking the next leap in your career, our courses and certifications will help you achieve your goals in SEO.

More than:

- **200** lessons
- **27 hours** of content
- **137** videos

and much more

Including:

- How does search work?
- Technical site audit
- Content strategy

... and **17 more** modules

WHAT OUR STUDENTS SAY

**"The Holy Grail of SEO"**

**"Best course of SEO ever"**

**"Mind blowing course"**

## The UK's leading SEO course

 **17,500+**
students enrolled

 **2,500**
certified students

Printed in Great Britain
by Amazon

13248147R00113